# Sam Houston, the Tallest Texan

# SAM HOUSTON

## The Tallest Texan

*by* WILLIAM JOHNSON

*Illustrated by* WILLIAM REUSSWIG

RANDOM HOUSE · NEW YORK

# Contents

*Sam Houston,*
*the Tallest Texan*

# 1: Tall as a Steeple

FEW OF THE MEN WHO SERVED WITH GENERAL SAM
Houston at San Jacinto knew exactly how tall he was.
But almost all agreed that he was taller than anybody
else.

Long after the battle of San Jacinto had made Texas
a free republic, and long after the free republic of
Texas had become a proud state of the Union, some old
men sat around a campfire and talked of Old Sam. They
either called him Old Sam or the General. To them
there was no other General.

"He looked as tall as that sweet gum tree," said one.
"Or maybe as tall as a church steeple."

3

*"I know how tall the General was."*

"He just had a way of looking tall," said another. "When they brought old Santy Anny to him as a prisoner at San Jacinty, there was Santy Anny standing stiff and straight in his Mexican monkey suit. And there was Old Sam on the ground on a dirty Indian blanket, his leg all busted up with shot and full of misery. And still Old Sam looked a head taller than Santy Anny, just a-laying there on his back, propped up on his elbow and his eyes flashing."

"Y'all ought to be bored for the holler horn," said a third, meaning that they were crazy. "I *know* how tall the General was. He wasn't but seven foot four."

They were, of course, all wrong.

Sam Houston was only about six and a half feet tall.

He was far taller than an average man but far short of a gum tree or a steeple. But he had a way of holding his body as straight as an arrow, even after it had been torn with battle wounds, so that he towered over other men.

And, more important, Sam Houston had a way of thinking, talking and acting that made him seem a giant.

Even when he was a very young man.

## 2: "Will We Be Brave?"

IN THE SPRING OF 1814 ENSIGN SAM HOUSTON MARCHED alongside his platoon of the 39th Regular Infantry Regiment. Under the leadership of General Andrew Jackson they were off to quell a Creek Indian uprising along the Tallapoosa River in the wilderness country. Led by a half-breed chief named Bill Weatherford, the Creeks had been attacking white settlements and killing settlers. It was believed they had received encouragement and possibly help from the British, with whom the United States was then at war.

The weather was warm for March. Spring was early that year. Redbud and dogwood were in bloom and

6

the young leaves on the oaks were bright green. Off through the trees Sam Houston could see the silver glint of the Coosa River. Above the sluff-sluff sound of marching feet he could hear redbirds calling and the harsh cries of bluejays.

Sam looked at his men. They were Tennessee re-cruits, as he was. They did not look like soldiers. They

*They walked like frontiersmen*

carried their .70 caliber smooth-bore rifles swung loosely under their arms as though they were going to shoot deer instead of Indians. They wore the official white pantaloons of the army but they looked as if they would be more comfortable in buckskins. Their walk was not the precise gait of soldiers, but of frontiersmen.

7

They covered the ground in an easy, swinging walk, toes in, one foot in front of the other.

A fellow-ensign fell in step beside Sam. He was another Blount County boy.

"They are a sorry-looking lot of soldiers, Sam."

"They are that," said Sam. "And after all those hours we spent drilling them at Knoxville. But they will be brave and good fighters, I warrant you. A little smoke and a little fire and a little blood."

There was a short silence between them. Then Sam threw back his head and laughed. His laugh was a roar, and tears came to his eyes. Soldiers in the column stared at the tall young ensign wonderingly.

The other ensign stared too. "What is it, Sam?" he asked.

Sam gasped for air and wiped his eyes on the sleeve of his jacket.

"Here I am talking about what it takes to make a soldier," he replied. "I've never been shot at, nor have I fired a shot in anger. I've never swung a sword except at weed stalks. I've tracked deer in the forest and trapped fish in the streams, but I've never tried to track or trap a man. I've measured bolts of calico in my brothers' store, but I've never measured a man for a sword thrust. And here I talk like an old soldier . . . this will happen, that will happen. I've learned to read the ancient poets, but can I read an enemy's mind? I

8

*Taking the silver dollar from the drumhead*

think not. Nor can you. But with God's help we will learn."

"That's right, Sam. Do you suppose—" His friend was worried about the thing that bothers all young soldiers going to battle for the first time.

"All we know for certain," said Sam, "is that we took the silver dollar from the drumhead and in that simple act became soldiers of the Republic, her defenders. We know Fort Hampton, the drill ground at Knoxville, the bivouac at Ten Islands, and we know this miserable wilderness track. They made us ensigns because we were big and strong, not because we were good soldiers. Only because we might become good soldiers. We know less of warfare than we know of the stars and what's beyond them. None of us is a soldier yet."

"Do you suppose, Sam, that we'll really get into a

fight this time? And do you suppose that we will be brave? They say the Creeks' war arrows have heavy, jagged heads that, once in your flesh, cannot be pulled free." The boy's voice and manner were worried.

Sam did not answer, and his friend thought perhaps he had asked the wrong question and that Sam was angry. Sam had strange ways. When he talked he talked a storm in a strange language that sometimes sounded like poetry and sometimes like something out of the hymn book. And then sometimes he would be silent for hours or days at a time. As silent as an Indian, and, like an Indian, you could not tell what was on his mind.

It was common knowledge in their home town of Maryville that Sam had lived a time with the Cherokees, speaking their language and wearing their dress.

As the shadows lengthened toward the east the regiment's friendly Cherokee scouts returned to the marching column. All day long they had prowled through the wilderness, a mile or so ahead of the main column, watching for enemy Creeks, watching for the crimson war club that meant the Creeks were on the warpath. Now they returned and reported that there was a good camp site just ahead.

The camp site was better than the 39th had been finding on its difficult route. There was a wide shelf on the north side of a gentle hill. The crown of the hill made a good post for observation toward the south. Below the shelf was a fast flowing spring where the men could fill their stomachs and their bottles with cool, clear water. And below this was a pool where they could wash the dust from their faces and soak their burning feet.

Sam shared a small fire of wind-fallen live oak sticks with his fellow-ensign. The wood crackled but made little smoke. The two ensigns took their rations of dried beef, speared them on green sticks and roasted them over the peppery smelling fire. Sam ate Indian fashion, biting into one side of the beef, holding the other side with his left hand and, with his razor-sharp, horn-handled hunting knife, sawing off a bite just in front of his nose. His friend put his chunk of meat between two slabs of cold corn bread.

Sam ignored the corn bread, but with his knife blade raked from the coals some charred roots that he had dug earlier out of the ground near the spring. He scraped the ashes from one root and bit into it. He tossed another to the ensign.

"Eat it. Good for you."

"What is it, Sam?"

"The Indian name would mean nothing to you. I guess that in our language you would call it 'food for braves.' In the old days when the Cherokee were a war-like nation the warriors ate this before they went on the warpath."

"Do you really believe those things, Sam?"

"When you live with the Indians, as I have done, you learn not to question the wisdom of the old men. It is not so with us. A white man can be old and foolish. An Indian only rarely. A foolish Indian dies young. I do not know whether this root will make us brave or not. The Cherokee are brave without it. But it is good to eat. Better than that cold corn bread."

The two ensigns watched the fire die. Sam took from his pack a red, blue and black Indian blanket, threw it around his shoulders and squatted on his heels close to the dying fire. The other ensign rolled himself in a homespun blanket. In the light Sam's chestnut hair looked black and the glow from the coals colored his face a rich copper shade. He looked like an Indian.

The wind was rising and sparks danced over the coals. The night sounds of the camp were quieting, there were the rattle of muskets being stacked and the groans of bone-weary men stretching themselves on the hard ground. Somewhere a whippoorwill cried.

"Many people hate and fear the cry of that bird," said Sam after a while. "They think it is an ill omen. But an old Indian I once knew said that it was good medicine for the warrior, that what the bird cries is 'all is safe, all is safe.' The bird will not cry thus if the enemy is near. Knowing this, the warrior can sleep in peace and build his strength for the battle. Good night."

His companion grunted sleepily. Sam looked at him for a moment and then turned back to the fire, continuing to stare into it.

# 3: The Horseshoe

THE NEXT DAY THE 2,000 AMERICAN TROOPS COM-
manded by General Andrew Jackson, among them the
39th Infantry including the platoon commanded by
Ensign Houston, moved on toward the enemy.

The Cherokee scouts reported to General Jackson
that the Creek Indians were prepared to make a strong
stand at Tohopeka, "the horseshoe." Tohopeka was a
wide bend in the Tallapoosa River in what is now
northern Alabama. The loop in the river, shaped like
a horseshoe, formed a peninsula pointed to the south.
Chief Bill Weatherford and his warriors had taken
their stand in this loop of land protected on the east,

13

south and west by the river. On the northern side they had built a high barricade of green logs and packed earth.

General Jackson, who was known as "Old Hickory" for his toughness, studied the situation. Then he sent General Coffee with a small body of American troops and some Cherokee scouts to cross the river below the horseshoe bend and approach the Creek stronghold from the south. Jackson then directed his two small cannons, which had been laboriously hauled through the wilderness, to be set up in position to fire on the barricade at the north.

Sam Houston watched the silent preparations. Around him the men of his platoon squatted on the ground and cleaned their rifles. From behind the barricade they could hear the Indians shouting. Sam Houston understood enough of the Creek dialect to know that the prophets were urging the warriors to drive the white man from the land.

Except for the distant clamor of the Indians the woods were quiet. Then, from far to the south, there was a single rifle shot.

"That's the signal," Sam said. "Coffee's men are in position."

Then from one of Jackson's two small cannons burst a puff of flame and smoke, and there was a roar in the woods. Before it died away the other cannon spoke.

14

The American troops threw themselves flat on the ground. Sam inched forward on his stomach toward the barricade. As the cannonading continued he watched closely and could see the cannon balls hit the barricade. They either buried themselves in the earthen chinking or bounced back harmlessly from the rubbery green logs. Now the Indians behind the barricade were firing at the men handling the cannons. Sam could hear the rifle balls whistling over his head. The American troops began firing at the Indians. But the Indians would appear above the barricade only for a second, long enough to aim and fire, and then disappear.

"We'll never make it this way," said Sam to his men. "Our cannon will never break that barricade. We are going to have to charge it."

A Cherokee scout approached at a run. His breech-clout and moccasins were dripping wet. He wore nothing else. He paused and in halting English asked where he might find General Jackson. Sam Houston answered him in Cherokee. The scout stared at Sam in amazement. Sam went on talking with him for a moment and then pointed toward the east. The scout continued on his way.

"What were you talking about?" one of the men in the platoon asked.

"That scout just came from Coffee's troops below the bend. They discovered Bill Weatherford's war canoes hidden in the brush at the river's edge. The scouts swam across and brought them back. Now the Creeks cannot escape. They are cut off. And Coffee is ready to attack them, using their own canoes."

The cannon ceased fire. Two American officers, one carrying a white flag, and an Indian interpreter crossed the clearing toward the barricade. Several Creeks raised their heads above the barricade and the two groups spoke together. Then the two officers and their interpreter turned and walked back to their own lines.

"Giving them a chance to get the women and children out," Sam explained.

Again there was silence among Jackson's troops except for the occasional rattle of a ramrod against a rifle barrel. Somewhere to the rear a man cried in pain as a comrade probed a wound for a rifle ball. But beyond the Creek barricade it was noisier than ever. The prophets were shouting: "The Great Spirit commands you. Raise your red sticks and drive the white enemy from our earth. Drive him beyond the mountains forever. If we are brave the Great Spirit will open the heavens and throw his wrath upon the whites."

"That screaming is a right scary sound," said one of Sam's men.

Sam paid no attention but went on whittling a cedar splinter with his hunting knife.

16

Now there was a long roll of drums from behind them. Major Lemuel Montgomery, a young officer whom Sam admired, shouted orders. Sam repeated the orders to his own platoon. With his sword in his right hand and beckoning to his men with his left, he rose and started for the barricade at a run, bending low to make a smaller target for the Indians. Now the woods were full of the sound and smell of gunfire. Rifle balls whistled and arrows hissed through the air.

Major Montgomery was the first to reach the barricade. He reached the top, turned to urge his men on, then spun around crazily as a rifle ball hit him in the head. He toppled backward.

Ensign Sam Houston was the second to reach the barricade. He gave a mighty leap and clambered to the top. He paused only long enough to make sure his men were following him. Then he gave another great leap and landed in the midst of the Indians.

Sam swung his sword about him and saw a painted warrior crumple to the ground with a gaping wound in his throat. Another Indian fell before him. Sam felt a burning in his leg but paid no attention to it. He looked back and saw that the soldiers of the 39th were pouring over the barricade as fast as they could come. The Indians were retreating slowly from the barricade. Many Indians had fallen. As he looked down at them Sam discovered the shaft of a war arrow sticking

*Major Montgomery toppled backward, and Ensign Sam
Houston leaped to the top of the barricade*

from his leg. In the fierceness of the fight he had been unconscious of the pain. Now at the sight of the arrow the pain struck him.

Sam leaned against a tree, bent, and tried to pull the arrow from his leg. But the barbed head was buried deep in his muscles and the agony robbed him of the strength to pull it free.

In the confusion of hand-to-hand fighting which was now going on all around him, he saw a lieutenant whom he knew. He shouted to him.

"Pull this blamed arrow from my leg, Lieutenant," he roared. "Please," he added.

"No, Ensign Houston. We'll get one of the men to take you back to the surgeon."

"Don't be an idiot, Lieutenant. There's a fight on. Pull this arrow out and be quick about it, or I'll club you with my sword."

"You are insubordinate, Houston. You . . ."

"You'll see whether I'm insubordinate or not!" Sam roared. He seized his sword and started to swing the flat side of it toward the lieutenant. His eyes had a wild look.

"All right, Houston. I was only thinking of your own good." The lieutenant's face was white. Sam stretched himself on the ground so that his leg muscles would be relaxed. The lieutenant took hold of the arrow shaft and pulled. The arrow hardly moved.

"Pull, man pull. Don't treat me like a baby," Sam ordered.

The man shook his head grimly. Seizing the arrow with both hands, he placed a knee against Sam's leg to brace himself and gave a mighty tug. The arrow moved a little. Sweat was running down Sam's face now, and his teeth were bared.

"Again," Sam ordered.

The lieutenant tugged again and the arrow came free, tearing a great hole in the flesh. Blood gushed out and Sam lay back with a groan. Now his strength was gone. The lieutenant called a soldier and sent him to search for a surgeon. He gave Sam a drink from his water bottle. Sam tried to get to his feet but fell back. "You go on with your men," he said, and closed his eyes. The sound of the fighting grew dim and the world seemed to be tilting up on end. For a moment there was complete blackness. He opened his eyes and saw the blood gushing from his leg. If that flow of blood kept on he would be done for. On his hands and one knee he crawled back to the barricade, dragging the wounded leg behind him. He crept over the barricade and collapsed on the other side.

A surgeon found him. He cut the torn trouser from the leg, cleaned the wound as well as he could and bound it tightly with strips of linen to stop the blood.

He covered the ensign with a blanket and left him there.

Sam's eyes were closed but he did not drift away this time. Clenching his fists against the pain, he remembered what his mother, a strong frontier woman, had told him as he prepared to march away from Maryville with the troops.

"Take this musket, my son," she had said. "Never disgrace it. Remember, I had rather all my sons fill one honorable grave than that one of them should turn his back to save his life. Remember, too, that while the door of my cabin is open to brave men, it is eternally shut against cowards."

## 4: No Chance to Live

SAM HEARD THE SOUND OF STEPS. HE OPENED HIS EYES. Two officers were standing over him. He recognized one by his thin face, his sandy hair and his stooped way of standing. It was General Jackson. Old Hickory.

"Are you Ensign Houston?" the general asked. Sam said he was.

"I'm told you were the first man on the barricade."

"I was the first live man on the barricade, sir. Major Montgomery preceded me, but he fell."

"It appears that you have fallen, too." The general smiled.

Andrew Jackson

"I shall be all right in a few minutes, sir."

"You are not to return to the fight, Ensign Houston. It is going well. You have done more than your part. We will have a litter take you to the rear."

Sam closed his eyes again and heard the general and his aide walking away. Go to the rear? No. And again he remembered his mother's parting words.

He struggled to his feet. Leaning on a stick, he once more approached the barricade.

While Sam had been lying on the ground the fighting had drifted south from the barricade. The ground was littered with Indian bodies. All had fought to death, spurning any offer of mercy. In many cases they finally were clubbed to earth with rifle butts.

Of the thousand Creeks who made the defiant stand in the horseshoe bend only a few hundred were left. Forced from their strong defensive position behind the barricade, they had retreated slowly southward. And at the southern tip of the peninsula Coffee's troops and their Cherokee allies had crossed the river in the Creeks' own canoes and stormed the small Indian settlement there, burning the cluster of Indian cabins. Thus the surviving Creeks were surrounded in the center of the peninsula. In such a hopeless situation they might have surrendered with honor. But not the Creeks. The Great Spirit had commanded them to fight to death against the palefaces. The prophets, their medicine men, urged the exhausted braves to continue the fight.

One of them, screaming and waving his crimson war club, shouted, "The Great Spirit will not desert us. He has promised to open the wrath of the skies upon our enemies if we are brave. Lo, my brothers, the Great Spirit sends us an omen," and he pointed with his war club to a great, gray rain cloud that now was creeping across the path of the afternoon sun.

A great shout went up among the surviving Indians. Now a white officer with an Indian interpreter approached them. General Jackson again was offering them surrender. Without waiting to hear the message the Indians set upon the two with clubs, knives and rifle butts. As they did so a few heavy drops of rain fell. This was their omen; the Great Spirit was coming to their aid. Screaming, the surviving Indians resumed the battle with the strength and fury of madmen.

24

From the top of the barricade Sam heard the pitch of the battle grow. Peering through the trees, he could catch glimpses of the unequal battle, three or four soldiers to one Indian. Knowing the Indian mind as he did, he knew the fighting would continue until every Indian had fallen. He slowly lowered himself inside the barricade and hobbled painfully toward the battle. The ground was wet with blood and the gently falling rain. His progress was slow and by the time he reached the troops it appeared that the fighting had ended. Searching, he found his own platoon. The men were weary, blood-stained and filthy with the dirt of battle. They dropped on the ground and stared vacantly at one another. Sam sank to earth beside his men, only to struggle to his feet again when he saw General Jackson approaching. All the weary soldiers arose as Old Hickory came near.

"I am calling for volunteers," said Jackson. "The Creeks are almost finished. But we must give them the final thrust. The only warriors left alive have barricaded themselves in that ravine," and the general gestured to the west.

"There are few of them, but they are in a firm position. We cannot train our cannon on them without endangering our own men. They must be dug out by frontal attack. It is a dangerous mission and I will not order any man to do it."

Sam Houston stepped forward unsteadily. "My platoon will go, sir."

Perhaps Jackson did not recognize Sam. Sam's face was drawn and white, and the forest had become gloomy and dark in the rain. Or perhaps Jackson had forgotten the young ensign he had ordered to the rear.

"Very well," said Jackson. "I wish you luck." He then gave a few brief orders.

Sam borrowed a musket, waved it at his men and once more started forward.

It was growing darker and the rain dripped from the trees. In the damp air the sharp smell of gunsmoke mingled with that of the burning Indian cabins. It was quiet except for the hum of insects and the evening cries of birds.

Sam tried to ignore the pain in his leg. As he hobbled forward he checked his musket load. A sword would have been of little use in getting the Indians out of the ravine. They had felled trees across the ravine, covering the top with branches, leaves and earth, but leaving a few openings around the side. Crouching low and peering through the gloom, Sam could see the glint of rifle barrels under the shelter and could hear the hum of Indian voices.

Heaving himself erect, Sam shouted to his men and stumbled clumsily toward the shelter, raising his mus-

26

ket as he went. A wild yell came from the ravine and the Indians began firing. Sam ignored it and stumbled on to within a few feet of the shelter. He raised his musket and fired into one of the openings.

Almost as he fired he was struck in the shoulder by two rifle balls at once. He twirled around and fell to the ground. Dimly he could hear the guns firing over him and the shouts of his men. Then everything faded out. He awoke once and felt himself being dragged over the ground. There was a great blaze in the sky. The stronghold had been captured and set afire. He had done his duty.

He awoke again later. He was stretched on a blanket and it was quiet. A surgeon, crouched near him, was speaking to someone.

"I have removed one of the rifle balls from his shoulder," the surgeon was saying. "There is no use removing the other. The boy cannot live anyway and it is useless to torture him. Better I should spend my time on cases that have a chance of living."

Sam closed his eyes and gritted his teeth, and again unconsciousness swept over him. Since no one held any hope for him he was not even given the usual comforts of the wounded—no water, no cover against the chilly night.

But Sam lived through the night and on through the

days during which he was hauled painfully through the wilderness to Fort Williams. Every jolt sent pain racing through his body. And as his fever built up, his mind drifted back over the days of his boyhood.

# 5: The Road to the Wilderness

THERE WAS ALWAYS AN IMPORTANT ROAD IN SAM Houston's life.

The one he was on now, the road back from the bloody battle of Tohopeka, marked the end of Sam's youth and the beginning of his life as a brave man.

There had been one important road before that. It was the road from Virginia, where Sam was born, to the wilderness of Tennessee, where he was to grow up.

Now, on the road back from Tohopeka, with every lurch of the litter Sam remembered the lurching of the immigrant wagon in which he, his widowed mother, his five brothers and three sisters had traveled to Tennessee.

*Everyone was headed for the wilderness of Tennessee or the land beyond*

That was when he was thirteen. His older brother John drove, flicking a long whip at the five-horse team. The trail up through the mountains and down into Tennessee was rough. When the sun shone there was heavy dust in the air. When it rained the trail became a pair of water-filled trenches in which the horses stumbled and the heavy wagon bogged.

Along the trail they passed big Conestoga wagons rolling along to the west and simple sledges with oaken runners being dragged along the route by teams of oxen. Now and then they would be passed by a finely dressed dandy on a prancing horse, saddlebags bulging and pistols at his side. Everyone was headed for the wilderness of Tennessee or the land beyond. They all wanted the same things: land and fortune in the raw new country, whether they came from New England, Pennsylvania or from Virginia, as the Houstons did.

As the family rode along, Elizabeth Houston, a tall, straight-backed woman with iron-gray hair, spoke with her children of where they had come from and where they were bound.

"Our people," she said, "have never been afraid of an enemy, have never been afraid to stand for what is right. Nor have they been afraid to move when the time

*"Your great-grandfather helped put the captain in chains"*

of disagreement or opportunity came. I want you, my children, to remember that always.

"All our people have been fighters. Not quarrelsome fighters but principled fighters. There were Houstons among the famed archers of Scotland. Houstons fought for John Knox and our religion, and when they were driven from Scotland they went to Ireland to live in freedom. Stop that, Samuel!"

Sam had been reaching from the wagon, grabbing tree limbs, holding them as the wagon moved and then letting them whip free. "Yes, ma'am," he said.

"Houstons fought at the siege of Derry, too, and when they were made to suffer for their beliefs they were not afraid to board ship and set sail for the New World.

"Your great-grandfather John Houston was not afraid. When the ship's captain tried to steal his gold, your great-grandfather and his friends seized the ship and brought it safely to Philadelphia although they knew little of sailing a ship. I have heard him tell the story. The captain was a vile and villainous man. Your great-grandfather helped put him in chains. This journey we make now is nothing compared with that adventure.

"Your dear father was a brave man, too. He was a captain in Morgan's Rifles in the War for Independence. He was courageous in combat and beloved by his men. And he was greatly honored by the commonwealth."

Sam did not remember his father very well. He had died only the year before, but Captain Samuel Houston had spent little time at home in the years before. He was away most of the time inspecting the Virginia militia, in which he was an officer. When he came home, a handsome man riding a good horse, he would have his sons stand at attention, like soldiers, to pass inspection. He had one of the old Negroes make wooden rifles for the boys, and he taught them the manual of arms. He told them many times of the way Morgan's men had beaten Tarleton at the battle of Cowpens.

Beyond that the captain took little interest in the children or in Timber Ridge plantation, which he had inherited from his father. While the boys went off to the Old Field school or down to Mill Creek to swim he would sit on the great square-pillared gallery and talk with Mrs. Houston. It was Mrs. Houston who ran the plantation. She would report to him on the cutting of wheat, the apple crop, on the illness of one of the slaves, and the old red cow's new calf. Then he would mount his horse and ride away on another inspection trip.

Sam admired his military-minded father and he rather liked his father's carefree attitude toward the plantation and all the work that had to be done to keep it going. But while he admired his father, he was devoted to his mother, knowing the heavy burden she carried. Young as he was, he knew that the plantation had to be sold, bit by bit, to keep the family dressed and fed, and he had watched the lines deepen in his mother's face. After his father's death, his mother grieved very little. She busily set about selling what

*Standing in the water was an Indian boy*

was left of the plantation and getting ready for the move to Tennessee. A few years earlier her husband had purchased a four-hundred-acre tract of wilderness land there.

"So," Mrs. Houston was saying, "we will have nothing to fear in the new country. There is much hard work ahead of us, but hard work does no harm."

Sam made a face.

"Mother," Sam's little sister Mary asked, "aren't there Indians who will attack us?"

"No, my child," said Elizabeth Houston, "in this part of Tennessee the Indians are peaceful. Cousin Jim Houston has a stockade on Nine Mile Creek, near the land that we will have. He built it when he came out from Virginia. In those days a stockade was necessary. Cousin Jim lost one of his own sons to the Indians and many of his neighbors were killed. But it has been nearly twenty years since they had any trouble with the Indians."

Indians, Sam thought. Now he might see some Indians. He had seen a few back in Rock Ridge County, lonely wanderers, separated from their tribes. Now he was going to real Indian country.

A few days later they arrived at Cousin Jim's stockade. Inside there was a house like the old Houston home at Timber Ridge except that it was roughly made of hand-shaped logs. There were slave houses, and outside was a stockade of sharpened timbers. Five miles farther on was the land on which Sam's family would make a new life. Cousin Jim showed it to them.

While Cousin Jim and Sam's mother talked of clearing away the trees, deepening the spring, building fences to keep deer out of the corn, finding a place for an orchard and vegetable patch, Sam wandered away and admired the view.

The land sloped toward the east, running down to a branch of Baker's Creek. From the slope Sam could see the Great Smoky Mountains in the east and south. He wandered along the creek. It was arched with trees, and the water was dark and clear.

Sam had a feeling someone was watching him. He pulled back a branch and looked upstream. Standing in the water was an Indian boy, about Sam's age. The boy stood still, staring at Sam. In his hand was a small fish, wriggling and shaking drops of water that sparkled in the tree-filtered sunlight.

"Hello," said Sam.

The boy said nothing. Slowly, without a sound and without taking his eyes from Sam, the boy stepped back and out of the creek. He put the fish in a reed basket and covered it with moss. Then he picked up some buckskin clothing from the bank, silently stepped back into the woods and vanished.

Later, while his brothers and sisters were helping their mother and friendly neighbors clear the Houston land, Sam would, when he could, slip away to the stream.

Weeks later he again came upon the Indian boy. The boy was driving fish into a crevice in the rocks and catching them with his hands.

Again Sam said, "Hello." This time he took his clasp knife that Cousin Jim had given him, and tossed it across the stream so that it landed near the Indian's clothes.

"It is for you," said Sam. "A gift."

The Indian said nothing. Sam turned and went back to where the family was working.

Another time Sam stole away, stretched himself on the bank of the stream and went to sleep. When he awoke the Indian boy was standing near him.

"Hello," said the Indian.

"Hello," said Sam.

"It is for you," said the Indian. "A gift." And he handed Sam a small fish, still alive and wriggling.

"Thank you," said Sam, taking the fish. "I am Sam Houston. Who are you?" The Indian said nothing, and again slipped away into the woods. Sam wrapped the fish in ferns, put it in his pocket and forgot about it until the next day when one of his sisters complained of the smell.

# 6: *Silver on the Drum*

THE HOUSTON LAND WAS CLEARED, CORN WAS
planted and the Houston house went up. It was not
so fine as the one in Virginia, although it was comfortable and had a good view toward the mountains. Now
all the efforts that had gone into clearing the land and
building the house went into the making of crops.

Sam loved his family and wanted to help them. Still,
work on the farm seemed dull and uninteresting. He
attended school for a while but he got more education
from the books he read outside of school. He particularly liked to read of the Greek and Roman heroes.
More and more often he wandered off into the woods,
a book in his pocket.

He became acquainted with the Indian boy from the creek. His name, Sam was surprised to find, was John Rogers, as English as Sam's own. John's mother was Cherokee, his father part Cherokee and part English.

After numerous meetings on the creek near the Houston home, John invited Sam to come see where he and his tribe lived. John had a canoe hidden in the willows at the edge of the Tennessee River. They paddled along the river until they came to an island. Here was a Cherokee village headed by Chief Oolooteka, or John Jolly, as he was known. Chief Jolly and the other Indians were grave and polite with Sam.

John Rogers had a brother, James, and a little sister named Tiana, a shy child who ran and hid from Sam. The Rogerses and their neighbors did not live in tepees but in well-built log cabins, many of them neater and cleaner than those of the white settlements that Sam knew. The women wove cloth, made clothing from cloth and skins, tended their gardens and their cows and chickens. The men had good rifles, spent their time hunting or in tribal councils, and carried themselves proudly. After the first visit Sam returned regularly and soon knew everyone in the settlement. He regarded the Rogers boys as brothers and Chief Jolly as a foster father.

Meanwhile the Houston family had begun to prosper. Sam's mother bought an interest in a small store in Maryville and Sam's brothers John and James went to work in it. Since Sam did not care for farm work they put him in the store also. Here he measured out beans and flour and corn and cut lengths of calico for the pioneer families of Blount County. He did not like it, but it was not as bad as work in the fields. Here, at least, he could talk to people. And at every opportunity he would go to visit his new Indian friends, always taking them some small gift from the store.

One day while he was working behind the counter Sam heard some men talking in front of the store.

"Them Houston boys is all right except young Sam," said one. "He's as lazy as a hound that leans against a fence to bark."

"No," said the other, "he's not lazy. He's just wild, a regular whip-around. He's just as likely to fly up the creek as not. They tell me he's always running away and visiting among them dirty thieving Indians."

Sam put down the shears with which he was cutting calico. He picked up his copy of Homer's *Iliad*, the story of the war between the Trojans and the Greeks. Then he walked out.

As he passed the men in front he glared at them and said, "If my friends in the forest were to spend all their time stealing they could not steal one half as much as the white man has stolen from them." Then, touching the greasy buckskin shirt one of the men was wearing, he added, "And as for being dirty, an Indian would not let his dog sleep on that shirt."

Then he turned and walked out of the settlement. That night he was back on the island in the Tennessee with his Cherokee friends, and this time he stayed. Chief Jolly gave him a pallet of blankets in his own house.

Sam adopted Indian dress and began to learn the Cherokee language. Chief Jolly gave him a Cherokee name, "Colonneh," meaning "The Raven." In Cherokee legend the raven had been a friend of man in the days when the Great Spirit was creating the world. The Great Spirit had placed fire in the bottom of a hollow tree. Man needed the fire and the raven tried to get it for him, flying down into the hollow tree and trying to bring out a burning ember. The raven scorched himself in the effort and remained black forever.

Sam saw, with satisfaction, that it was the women who did the work in the little corn fields and the peach orchards. The men hunted or fished or spent their time in councils, games or just conversation. With John and James Rogers, Sam learned to track deer in the forest, learned how to snare rabbits and catch fish in his hands or with simple nets. He learned the green corn dance and the Cherokee ball game. At night he would sit with the men in the council chamber and hear the wise talk of old men.

One day he was lying on the river bank reading from his beloved *Iliad*. He heard the sound of a paddle and rose to see his brothers John and James approaching the island in a canoe.

"Sam, you must come home," said John. "You must stop living like a savage and come home to your family and duties."

"Go away and leave me alone," said Sam. "Please tell our mother that I love her with all my heart. But I have, here in the forest, two Indian brothers named, as you are, John and James, who are more nearly my brothers than you have ever been. I would far rather measure deer tracks with them in the forest than measure calico with you in the store in Maryville."

Sam won the argument and the brothers went away and left him. But periodically Sam's love for his mother would draw him home. He would stay for a while and then return to the Indians. On one of those visits he taught school for a term in order to raise money for gifts to his Indian friends. In all he spent almost three years of his youth with the friendly Cherokees.

Meanwhile back in Maryville the talk was all of the new war with the British. Tennesseans, like other Americans of the frontier, recognized the British as an obstacle to further westward expansion. Too, they were certain that the British were stirring up the hostility of some Indian tribes toward the American colonizers.

Once back in Maryville Sam stood with his friend Willoughby Williams and watched a troop of regular soldiers drilling in an open field. They were experienced soldiers and wore smart uniforms with white breeches. The drill had been arranged to attract recruits for the regular army. The drill sergeant placed a drum on the ground and scattered a handful of silver

*Sam was reading from his beloved* Iliad

dollars on the drumhead. To enlist, all that a man had to do was step up and take a dollar from the drumhead.

Sam turned to Willoughby Williams. He was smiling.

"I've watched our militia drill," he said. "And they are a bunch of sorry ragtags. I never had any inclination to be a militiaman. Most of them are pure no account. But I think I'd like to be a regular soldier, wear a good uniform and fight for my country. I think I will join."

Sam stepped forward to pick up his silver dollar. As he did Sam heard someone in the crowd laughing.

A voice said: "There's Sam Houston, the Indian lover, going to be a soldier. What will he do if he has to fight Indians? Sit down and cry?"

Sam stepped up to the man, stared him in the eye and said:

"You will hear of me."

Sam remembered all this now in the litter coming back from the battle of Tohopeka. They would hear of him all right, whether he lived or died.

# 7: *"You Can Help Us"*

No ONE EXPECTED SAM TO RECOVER FROM HIS
Tohopeka wounds. No one except Sam himself. He
was left at Fort Williams with no medical attention.
When the troops at Fort Williams were demobilized
they rigged a horse litter and carried the young ensign
to his home. It had been almost two months since he
was wounded, during which time he had had little care.

But after a little while at home, gathering strength
under his mother's care, he journeyed to Knoxville
for medical attention. The doctor in Knoxville did not
want to take the case. The patient was too near death.

"You will change your mind," said Sam. He took a

room in Knoxville and rested for a few weeks. Then he returned to the doctor and said, "See, I am still alive. Now will you take my case?"

The doctor did and Sam began to recover. He managed to rejoin his regiment in the year 1815. He was promoted to second lieutenant and assigned to New Orleans. To get there he and two fellow officers bought a small boat and began floating down the rivers, first the Cumberland, then the Ohio and finally the Mississippi.

Sleeping under the stars at night and drifting lazily along under the warm sun by day, they had much time for talk and reading, both of which Sam loved. They talked mostly of the West. This was the way many people were beginning to go to the West, floating down the Mississippi and then ascending either the Arkansas or the Red River. There was a future out there, Sam and his friends decided, just as their parents, in Virginia, had talked of the future in Tennessee.

Sam was to recall this conversation later.

He was sitting one day, some years afterward, in his law office in Lebanon, Tennessee. Here he had settled after leaving the army. He had begun to do well with the law. Through the friendship of General Jackson, his old commander, he had been appointed adjutant general of the Tennessee militia. "Old Hickory," as almost everyone knew Jackson, was living on his Nashville plantation, not far from Lebanon. Houston went there often to see him.

On this day Houston was working on his militia rolls. A man walked into his office. He was well dressed, with a beaver hat and a silk waistcoat. His face was tanned a deep brown and his hair was black and shining.

"Sam, you don't remember me," said the visitor.

"No, I am afraid that I do not."

"You don't remember Baker's Creek and the island in the Tennessee? And reading to James and me from the *Iliad,* all about the Greek and Trojan warriors?"

"John Rogers! I didn't know you in that getup." Sam threw his arm around John's shoulders and pushed him into a chair.

"I am trying to help my people. To do this I have to go among the white men and dress and behave like a white man."

"What is wrong with your people—and my people?"

"Everything. It is not your fault, Sam, but you remember having come to us, John Jolly's people, to tell us that we should exchange our lands in Tennessee for lands in the Arkansas territory that the government would give us?"

Houston replied that he did. It had been one of his last missions before leaving the army. He had been sent because he not only spoke the Cherokee language, but was trusted by the Cherokees, who regarded him as one of them.

"Sam, you remember in our religion, in the tales the old man told us, the West was always the Dark Land, the home of the Dark Spirits. Good came from the East and evil from the West.

"Well, it is a dark land. The lands that were promised us are not as fertile as they were supposed to be, nor as large. Not as good by far as the lands we gave to the government for the white settlers. But it is not just the lands. The agent sent out by the government to see to our needs has not done so. My people, our people, need money for cattle and tools, money for supplies to carry us until we have more land cleared and more crops. Money was promised us for the cleared land we had to leave behind in Tennessee. The agent cheated us. Many of us have received no money at all and few have received all that was due them. We have forced this evil agent to leave us, but we may get a worse one.

"Why do you not become the Indian agent? General Jackson would help you get the appointment."

"How can you be so sure of that?"

"Sam, we were at Tohopeka, the battle of the horse-shoe. My brother James and I were scouts for your forces. You did not know this because we Cherokees kept to ourselves. But we knew you were there. We

48

knew of your bravery and of what General Jackson said of you after the fighting."

"I didn't know you were there. I wish I had known. But what did General Jackson say?"

"He said: 'This boy will go far, if he lives, and will do great things for his people.' We are your people, Sam. Will you try to get the appointment as agent?"

Houston said he could not answer immediately, that he would have to think it over.

"And I tell you this, Sam," his friend went on. "While the West has been a dark and evil land for the Indian, it is a bright land for the white man, a country that some day will be rich and powerful. If you come there you can help us, and maybe also help yourself."

Houston nodded and remembered the days floating down the river toward New Orleans, talking and dreaming of the land that lay to the west.

That night he walked the streets of Lebanon, disturbed by John Rogers' report on what was happening to the Cherokees, his people, and wondering what he could do about it. He made up his mind that he should go to their aid.

The next day he saddled his horse and rode to The Hermitage to see General Jackson. He explained the matter to Jackson. Jackson nodded and said if that was what Houston wanted he would write a letter to Washington recommending his appointment.

# 8: *Westward Again*

JACKSON'S WORD WAS ENOUGH TO MAKE THE APpointment as Indian agent certain. But the mails were slow, and by the time official notification reached Houston he was involved in other matters and was forced to decline.

He had been persuaded to run for prosecuting attorney of the Nashville district. It was the beginning of the first of the two political careers he was to have in his lifetime. He not only had a record as a war hero but was also personally popular. He won easily. Next he was elected a major-general in the Tennessee militia and, in the year 1823, he was elected United States congressman from Tennessee.

*Houston was personally popular*

He was a spectacular figure in Washington. Tall and good-looking, he dressed stylishly. Almost always he had a bright Indian blanket thrown around his shoulders as a reminder of his Indian days. Many people thought he actually was part Indian.

Once a young French diplomat expressed a desire to see this Congressman from Tennessee who he had heard really was an Indian in disguise. Houston's friends arranged the appointment and Houston prepared to receive the young diplomat in his hotel room. When the Frenchman reached the room Houston was sitting on the floor, his face painted, wearing nothing but a loincloth. He was gnawing at a beef bone. He asked in the Cherokee language what the young man

wanted, scowling at him. The frightened diplomat
fled down the hall.

Usually Houston's manners were of the best. He was
courtly with ladies and a good companion among men.
But brave as he was, he disliked violence.

When, during a trip back to Tennessee, he was chal-
lenged to a duel, he tried by all honorable means to
ignore the challenge. When this was impossible, he retired to a farm to practice pistol shooting. He followed
General Jackson's advice and clenched a bullet in his
teeth to steady his aim.

On the day of the duel he arose long before daylight
to melt his lead and mold his bullets. While he was
molding one a dog barked and a rooster crowed. This,
Houston decided with an Indian's feeling for good and
evil signs, was a good omen. He made two small marks
on the bullet he was molding, one for the dog and one
for the rooster. This would be his lucky bullet. It was.
When, in the gray morning light, the two men paced
off the distance, whirled and fired, his opponent's shot
went wild and Houston's was true. The man did not
die, but it took many months for him to recover. And
during this time Houston, bothered by what he had
been forced to do, was his most constant well-wisher.

Houston left Congress to return to Tennessee and
run for the governorship. He was elected and gov-

erned well. His old friend General Jackson had been
elected to the Presidency and this helped make Houston one of the most prominent men of the frontier
country. His personal popularity was becoming almost
as strong as that of General Jackson himself. In 1829 he
married a Tennessee belle, a girl much younger than
himself. She was from a prominent family, and the family was anxious to be linked with the rising political figure. There was talk that Sam Houston might some day
be President of the United States.

The marriage took place near the end of Houston's
first term as governor. Urged by all his friends, he
decided to run for a second term.

One of his friends was Willoughby Williams, who
had been a boyhood friend in Maryville. Williams had
watched Sam enlist and had been the first to greet him
when he was carried back from Tohopeka. Now Williams was sheriff in Nashville. He was devoted to
Houston both as a friend and a hero.

Late in the campaign Sheriff Williams took his horse
and made a tour of small towns in western Tennessee
to test Houston's popularity and get an idea how the
election would come out. The results were encouraging.
It appeared that it would be impossible for Houston to
lose the election. Sheriff Williams sang as he rode back
to Nashville. It was a song that was being sung then in

*His opponent's shot went wild and Houston's was true*

the traveling minstrel shows, an old soldiers' song about General Jackson's victory over the British at New Orleans:

> *Old Jackson he was wide awake,*
> *And was not scared at trifles,*
> *For well he knew what aim to take,*
> *With our Kentucky rifles.*

Williams hummed a few bars for which he had forgotten the words and then bellowed out:

> *For every man was half a horse*
> *And half an allygator—Oh, Kentucky!*
> *The hunters of Kentucky.*

The sheriff was still singing as he rode up to the Nashville Inn where Houston was making his headquarters.

A crowd was gathered in front of the inn. The sheriff waved at friends, swung himself from his horse and slapped the dust from his clothes with his hat.

"Governor Houston will be governor again," he said to some acquaintances. "No doubt about it—say, what's got you? What's the matter?" The men's faces were long and they were saying nothing. The sheriff walked into the hotel. The public room was crowded with little groups of men talking together in low voices. The sheriff started for the stairs when someone laid a hand on his shoulder. A friend asked, "Have you heard the news?" The sheriff said that he had not.

"Sam and his wife had some kind of a bust-up," the man said. "Nobody knows for certain what it was about. Some of the boys around here say that Mrs. Houston married Sam not because he was Sam but because he was Governor Houston and might some day be President Houston. And you know how proud Sam is. Anyway, they say that when Sam found out about it somehow he lost his temper, lost it bad. But nobody knows for sure, as I said. Neither Sam nor Mrs. Houston will talk to anybody. She's gone home to her folks and Sam just stays up there in his room. They say that Sam's going to resign as governor and leave the state."

Late that night the sheriff was summoned to Houston's room. Houston was sitting before the fireplace, his legs outstretched, going through stacks of letters and papers, looking at them briefly, his face grim, and burning them in the grate.

"Hello, sheriff," Houston said, his voice calm. "Sit down and witness an interesting sight. Here you see Sam Houston, major-general of the Tennessee militia, congressman from Tennessee, governor of the great state of Tennessee, preparing to become Sam Houston, private citizen. I am leaving, resigning, exiling myself from the state I have loved and the state I have bled for."

The candle flickered and the fire died. The two old friends sat and talked far into the night. Houston talked of the times in the army, talked of Jackson, talked of his days in Washington, but never mentioned the quarrel with Mrs. Houston. Nor did Sheriff Williams ask him about it.

The next morning the two of them walked out of the Nashville Inn. It was a beautiful spring morning. There was a cockfight going on in the vacant area next to the three-story hotel. Carriages with Negro drivers slowly wheeled through the streets. Here and there men in frontier clothes slouched along in their easy walk with their rifles carried loosely under their arms. Everywhere there were small groups of people, talking together in low voices and staring at Houston. In all the gossip about Houston and his wife some men around the town had accused Houston of cowardice and had boasted of what they would do to him if they ever caught him in public. Now no one stirred. Some took off their hats and spoke politely to the governor. Houston returned their greetings solemnly.

The pair walked down Market Street, sloping to the

Cumberland River. There a steamer, the *Red Rover,* was tied. Houston, followed by Williams, walked up the gangplank.

"Sam," said Williams, "I know that you are a man of honor and a gentleman. But don't you think you should explain to your friends why you are leaving? And what it was that happened? Many untruths will be told about you, and your friends will suffer, knowing them to be untruths but having no way to fight them."

"I hope my friends never suffer because of me, Williams. But I cannot talk now, nor will I ever. I hope that in the West I can make another life. If fame comes to me again, that is well. If it does not, that is as it must be, and all this will be forgotten."

Williams shook his hand and walked sadly down the gangplank.

For hours afterward, as the boat worked its way toward the junction of the Cumberland and the Ohio, the tall man stood at the rail, staring at the brown water.

# 9: *Invitation to a Treasure Hunt*

A WEEK LATER HOUSTON WAS WALKING ALONG THE waterfront of Cairo, a noisy river town where the Ohio joins the Mississippi. A gang of Negroes chanted a work song as they unloaded one river boat and loaded another, and a driver shouted curses at a team of stubborn mules hitched to a loaded wagon.

Houston had a week's beard on his face and a dark beaver hat pulled low over his eyes. He rubbed the bristling beard and gazed along the river front, looking for something.

At the water's edge was a small flatboat. It was a shallow, square-ended scow. Forward there was a

roofed-over shelter under which two large hounds lay
sleeping. Amidships was a pile of hardened clay on
which the remains of a fire smouldered. In the stern a
man in mud-stained homespun was whipping some
rope ends.

"My friend," said Houston, "I want to go to the Arkansas territory. Can you take me?"

"Ben Button is your servant for a consideration,"
said the boatman. "That I can do well. This here pala-
tial craft will take you to Arkansas territory. Where
d'you have a mind to go? Helena? Arkansas Post? Little
Rock?"

Houston said he wanted to go to Little Rock.

"Ben Button's your man and will see you there,
Guv'nor."

Houston started at being addressed as "Guv'nor."
He had thought he was traveling incognito. Possibly
the man was only using it as a polite form of address.
But when Houston looked at Button's sharp eyes he
realized it was more than that.

"You needn't jump, Guv'nor. The little bits of whiskers don't fool nobody. The captain of the *Red Rover*
told most everybody on the waterfront. He's headed on
down the river and within a month they'll be looking
for you all the way from New Orleans to Saint Looey.
Me, I don't care whether you're guv'nor or not. If
you're a mind to go to the Arkansas territory and you

can pay me a little for my corn meal, beans and side-meat, we'll go. I've got tackle for fishing, guns for shooting and two handsome dogs to tree bear and other varmints if you've a mind for a little sport. And if it makes you feel any better I'll call you general instead of guv'nor."

Houston smiled at the man's good humor and the deal was made. The next morning before dawn he boarded the flatboat, stowed away his baggage and Button pushed the boat out into the river. Where the currents of the two rivers boiled together it was rough and the current was swift. Button skillfully steered the boat through the fast water and then poled it easily along in the shallow water and the eddies near the shore. He would not have to use the oars until they began to ascend the Arkansas River. The spring sun was bright and hot. The leaves of the willows and cottonwoods were bright green. Grass was springing through the sand and mud at the water's edge, rich soil brought down by the late winter floods.

Button baited some hooks with pork fat and trailed the lines behind the boat. He hauled in two giant catfish. He cleaned them quickly, throwing the entrails to the two "varmint hounds." Then he built a fire of oak chips on the mound of clay, slapped the slabs of catfish into a black skillet and put it on the fire. He mixed corn meal with water in a Dutch oven and put it

in the fire. All the while he kept an eye on the river
and the boat's direction, pushing with his pole occasionally to keep from going aground.

After a while he shouted, "Grub's ready. If you
don't eat it I and the hounds will."

Houston ate his first good meal since leaving Nashville. Later, stretched on the deck with a hand shading
his eyes from the sun, he told Button, "It wasn't long
after our fight at Tohopeka that I came down this river
for the first time, headed for duty at New Orleans. We
floated along on the river as we are doing now, and we
talked of going west. I knew I would do it some day. I
probably should have done it then, or as soon as I
could get out of the army. Now I have to start in at the
age of thirty-five, start all over again. But the West is
great, Button, and it will be greater. . . ." His voice
faded and he slept in the sun.

Some nights they slept on the boat, rolled in blankets on the deck. Other nights they would camp on the
river bank, watching a campfire and listening to the
night cries of birds. Some nights they took the hounds
and went hunting in the wooded bottom lands. One
morning they brought in an eight-point buck and on
another a small black bear. Their diet of catfish and
corn bread was varied with bear and venison steaks and
stew. Other nights Button would sit by the fire and

*Jim Bowie shook hands with Houston*

tell great stories of huge fish and alligators in the bayous, of river pirates and hidden treasure.

At the Arkansas territory river town of Helena the boatman put in for supplies. While he went in search of beans and meal, Houston waited in the boat. He looked up to see Button and a big sandy-haired man shuffling down the steep dirt path to the boat.

"This here's a man wants to see you, Gen'ral," said Button. "Don't get me wrong. I didn't tell him who you are. He just up and asked me where my boat was. But he's a good man. He hasn't killed more than two or three men, and they needed killin'."

The stranger stepped on the boat and shook hands with Houston. In his belt was a big broad-bladed knife.

"I'm Jim Bowie, General. I heard you were coming. I'm proud to know you, and having said that I'll come right to my point.

"I hear you are headed west. I'd be proud to have you come along with me. I've been out in the Texas country for a while. The Mexicans aren't as bad as people will tell you. I get along with them right well and I can speak that Mexican language. I have some ideas for that country that I need a good partner for, and I will need some capital. And I know how to get that, too. I'm on the trail of a hidden mine in the San Saba country. There are lots of Spanish silver and gold bars stored in that mine and a lot more ore than was ever taken out of it. The Lipan Indians know me and they will lead us there. We get that and we will have a stake for more operations, or maybe we wouldn't have to work at all if that treasure's as rich as I hear. Anyhow I'd like to have a man like you come along and work with me."

Houston listened to Bowie's speech with amazement. He remembered the name now. Bowie was a Tennessean, too. He had fought duels, been accused of piracy and smuggling, and, they said, rode alligators and speared wild cattle for amusement. He had been on the Long expedition that tried to set part of Texas free from Mexico. He was a fighter, but a respected man.

64

"I'm flattered, Bowie," he replied, "and what you describe is a great temptation. I'm sure I could do no better than cast my luck with yours. But this is a difficult time for me. I want to go for a while among my old friends, the Cherokees, to rest and collect my thoughts. After that we shall see."

Bowie nodded and said that he understood.

"But I'll tell you this, Bowie," Houston continued, "from what I hear of Texas, the treasure is not hidden away in a mine. It is there in the open under God's great sky, with plenty of freedom for a man to move around."

Bowie nodded again and told Houston of the vast land to the west, the great grassy plains, the rich bottom lands along the rivers, the abundance of game and the mildness of the climate. They sat up all night talking of the new land. Bowie did not leave until Button shoved off his boat at dawn.

During the days it took them to descend the Mississippi to the mouth of the Arkansas and ascend the Arkansas to the territorial capital of Little Rock, Houston thought often of Bowie and his talk of Texas. He promised himself that some day, not too far away, he would get to that fabulous land.

## *10: Black Fox and the Log*

AT LITTLE ROCK HOUSTON SAID GOODBYE TO THE boatman, bought a horse and took off toward the northwest, following the Indian trails along the Arkansas River.

He stopped in the river front settlements of Dardanelle to buy supplies. Having bought them, he rested for a while in front of the trader's store. An old Indian was trudging up the road carrying a sack of corn on his shoulders. A trapper who had just sold his last pack of furs for the season and was drinking up his profit, approached from the other direction.

"Hey, you danged old Injun, get off the road and let

a white man pass," the trapper shouted. The Indian paid no attention but plodded ahead with his heavy load.

"I told you to git off the road," the trapper roared. As the Indian passed he drew back his moccasined foot and gave the old man a tremendous kick. The old man fell and the corn spilled over the roadway.

Houston walked over to the man.

*The trapper went flying face downward in the dust*

"May I have a word with you?" he asked.

"Huh?" said the trapper. Houston was standing very erect and staring straight at the man.

"You will get down in the road," he said, "and pick up the man's corn. For every grain that is left in the road in one hour's time I will give you one kick such as you gave him."

"I'm not going to do any such danged thing for a danged Indian," said the trapper.

With his left fist Houston tapped the trapper in the stomach. The trapper bent over with the blow. As he did so Houston stepped to one side, lifted a heavily booted foot and kicked the man in the backside. The trapper went flying face downward in the dust.

"Pick up the corn, I said," Houston repeated. Then, speaking softly in Cherokee, he went to the old Indian and helped him to his feet.

"It is a rare thing that you speak our language," said the old man. "It is even rarer for a white man to show concern for one of us."

"I am one of you," said Houston, "by adoption if not by birth. I go now to join my foster father, John Jolly, in his new wigwam."

"Yes," said the Indian. "His new wigwam. Not long ago he lived a day's ride from here, no more. Then the white man made us move again. I am the last here and I do not stay long. Come, I will show you something."

While the trapper, muttering to himself, began picking up the corn, Houston walked up the road with the old Indian.

The Indian pointed to a grove of oak trees near the river bank. In the center was a clearing.

"Here, under these council oaks," he said, "the Indian chieftains and headmen and your government

people held a meeting some years ago, eight or ten, I
do not remember. But I remember this:

"On this log sat the officer of your Arkansas territory. Beside him sat our chief, Black Fox.

"Black Fox would move close to the officer on the
log and ask him politely if he could move a little farther and make a little more room. The officer would
move. Then, after a pause, Black Fox would ask him if
he would move still a little farther. Each time the officer would do as Black Fox asked until, finally, he
came to the end of the log. Then he turned to Black
Fox and complained that there was no other place
to go.

"Black Fox looked at him, smiled and said, 'Now you
know how it is with us. The white man has asked us to
move and to move a little more and a little more again
until we have no place to go.' "

Houston stood silently staring at the log for a minute
and then suggested that they go back and see if the
trapper had finished picking up the corn. He gave the
old Indian his corn and told him good-bye.

The next morning Houston boarded a packet boat
and continued on up the Arkansas River.

"*Each time the officer would do as Black Fox asked until,
finally, he came to the end of the log*"

## 11: *The Raven Comes Home*

THE LITTLE PACKET BOAT LABORED SLOWLY UP THE
Arkansas, past Fort Smith, once a military establish-
ment but now temporarily abandoned and occupied
mainly by trappers, traders and whiskey runners.
Towed behind the packet boat was a barge loaded with
trading goods, bolts of calico, butternut cloth and
woolens, seed grain, tools, farming implements and
lead for bullets. At the trading posts these would be
exchanged for fur skins, the last of the winter's haul. At
clearings along the river there were Indian cabins.
There were cattle and chickens and small fields under cultivation.

The boat finally reached Webber's Falls, the end of navigable water on the Arkansas. Here, where the packets ended their run, a half-breed Cherokee trader named Watt Webber made his headquarters.

While the boat was being secured to a pair of ancient cottonwood trees, a crowd gathered on the bank. All were Indians and most of them were Cherokees. Houston left the boat and made his way through the crowd. The Indians smiled at Houston and their children tugged at his clothing.

An older Indian approached him. He was tall for an Indian. Despite his age his back was straight and his body still strong.

"Colonneh, my son," he said to Houston.

"Oolooteka, my father," said Houston, and they embraced. It was John Jolly, his foster father in the days of his youth.

"We had word of your coming," said John Jolly. "Eleven winters have come and gone since last we met. I have been told that you were a great chief among your people and that a dark cloud has crossed your path. It was the work of the Great Spirit. If it has brought grief to you I am sorry. But it is good fortune for me and our nation for it has brought you to us. We have great troubles and you have been sent to give us help. My wigwam is yours and my people are your people."

A short horseback ride took them to John Jolly's lodge. It was a long log house, well built and new. At a hitching rail, a peeled sapling strung between two oak trees, were a dozen fine horses. In a stick corral at one side were some milk cows. On a hilly slope beyond the house some beef cattle grazed. Behind the house two Negro servants were tending a pit fire over which a half of a beef carcass was roasting. Squatting on the ground around the fire and under the trees were Indians. Some wore buckskin hunting shirts and leather leggings as John Jolly did, but more of them were dressed as farmers.

Houston went from one to another in the group, greeting some by name, embracing old friends and speaking gravely to others, picking up dark-skinned youngsters and holding them in the air to admire them.

The feasting began in the morning and lasted all day. Besides the beef there were game, venison and wild turkey, potatoes and savory roots roasted in the ashes, parched corn, fruits and nuts saved from the winter. As the men finished eating, they made speeches. Finally it was Houston's time.

"The Cherokees have always tried to live with the white man and by the white man's law," he said. "When the Cherokees have made an agreement they have lived up to it. The white man has not always done so. Eleven years ago, under army orders, I came among

73

you, my people, to persuade you to move west to the Arkansas territory. This you did under my foster father's leadership. You settled on the land in the Arkansas territory that was assigned to you. It was not good land, but it was better than this. It was good enough for white men to want it. The government's promises were not kept. The indemnity money was not paid. And finally, my people were ordered to move on from that land to this. You were promised vast hunting lands to the west. But those lands are roamed by savage Indians, the plains Indians who dislike the Cherokees as much as they dislike the white man. Thus, my people, you are pushed from the East by the white man and pushed from the West by the red man. The plains Indians kill you; the white man cheats you. Colonneh, The Raven, your son and brother, has come among you to live and make his home. Whatever strength there is in The Raven's arm, whatever courage there is in his heart is yours to command. The Raven has come home."

## 12: Cherokee Ambassador

HOUSTON DISCARDED HIS TENNESSEE CLOTHES and put on a buckskin shirt and leggings like his foster father's.

"I am no longer a white man in anything but color," he told John Jolly. "I shall no longer think as a white man. I have left those who were my people and joined those who are."

He began renewing acquaintances among the Cherokees. He also visited other Indian settlements, the Creeks and the Choctaws among them, listening to their grievances and promising to do what he could to help them. He was, however, against any warfare.

When some of the younger Indians proposed that they go on the warpath against the Pawnees and the Comanches who opposed them in the west, Houston firmly resisted it.

He began to be recognized as the most powerful single man among all the Indians who were being forced westward. Back in the East there were rumors that Houston planned to mobilize an Indian army to march into Texas and free it from Mexico's rule. Houston's old friend General Jackson, now the President, had long wanted to join Texas to the United States. Efforts had been made to persuade Mexico to cede Texas to the United States. Attempts had been made to purchase it. There had been much talk of armed conquest. But for the moment President Jackson wanted to pursue only peaceful means. He wrote to Houston and placed him on his honor not to undertake any such project.

Whether Houston had planned it or not, Jackson's request was law as far as he was concerned. In addition to this Houston was stricken, soon after, with malaria. Lying on a corn-shuck pallet in John Jolly's lodge and covered with a buffalo robe, he suffered burning fever and terrible chills. A Cherokee medicine man performed his rites over him, spitting a mixture of bark and water on his body and chanting prayers to the spirits of the mountains, the forests and the whirl-wind to come and drive away the illness.

When he finally recovered he went to a meeting of the Cherokee clans at which the Cherokee agent, Major E. W. DuVal, was to pay, in gold, the indemnity money owed the Cherokees by the government. Traders from all over the Arkansas territory were there to sell the Indians goods in exchange for their gold—blankets, flasks of gunpowder, knives and, secretly, whiskey, which was not supposed to be sold to Indians.

The agent announced that the government had been unable to deliver the gold in time for the payment. Instead there were certificates of payment with which the Indians could collect their gold later.

The Indians had little use for the pieces of paper. The tradesmen, recognizing this, offered to discount the certificates. They would accept a certificate worth twenty dollars, and give the Indian as little as two dollars in trade. Agent DuVal himself had set up a trading post to sell the Indians goods for heavily discounted certificates. Houston, watching the systematic way in which the Indians were being cheated, promised himself he would take care of DuVal if the opportunity ever came. It came sooner than he expected.

At the next meeting of the tribal council Houston

was adopted as a member and made a citizen of the Cherokee nation. As such, he was chosen to head a delegation going to Washington to present the Indians' grievances to the federal government.

John Jolly sent him with a letter addressed to President Jackson:

Great Father:

My son The Raven came to me last spring. At my wigwam he rested with me as my son. He has walked straight, his path is not crooked. He is now leaving me to meet his white father General Jackson and look upon him, and I hope he will take him by the hand and keep him as near to his heart as I have done. He is beloved by all my people.

The first night on the trail Houston and his companions camped near the home of the Indian agent, DuVal. DuVal invited them to his house. Once there he drew Houston aside and showed him a letter he had received.

"General," he said, "a friend tells me that you are going to Washington to make charges against me as Indian agent. I cannot believe that this is true. I intend to tell my friend that it is a lie."

"I would not do that, Major," said Houston. "For then you would be guilty of a lie. Among the things I hope to accomplish in Washington is a report to the government concerning the dealings you and other agents have had with the Indians." He looked DuVal straight in the eye.

DuVal turned white. "Would you be so kind," he asked, "as to list the charges you intend to make?"

"Gladly," Houston replied. Taking paper and quill pen he listed the charges—profiteering, cheating, breaking faith. When he had finished he made an exact copy, had DuVal initial it to show that he had read it.

"Now you know where I stand," Houston said. Calling to his two Cherokee companions he walked out of DuVal's house, ignoring the agent's eager offer of hospitality. Houston and the two Indians camped and slept on the trail.

Six weeks later they reached Washington. Houston still wore his Indian attire, yellow leggings, breach-clout, hunting coat and a bright blanket around his shoulders. He attracted much attention in the streets of the capital city. He wore the same dress when he went to call on President Jackson in the Executive Mansion, which people were beginning to call the White House. Old members of Washington society who had long sneered at Jackson for his friendship with rough and ready old friends from his frontier and army days now criticized him for being friendly with "a savage."

Jackson and Houston paid no attention to such criticism. Houston presented his evidence against the dishonest Indian agents and Jackson saw to it that they were dismissed from the service.

It was spring when Houston returned to John Jolly's lodge. It was time, he decided, to have a home of his own. He selected a site on the Verdigris River, about thirty miles north of John Jolly's lodge. He hired workmen to fell trees and cut logs for a sturdy house. He had the land cleared and planted an apple orchard. He secured goods and set up a trading post. Tiana Rogers, a widow and sister of his old friends the Rogers brothers, brought her children and came to keep house for him. Houston enjoyed having a comfortable home and having children around.

Operating the trading post was just as tiresome as clerking in the store back in Maryville had been. He employed a clerk to handle the trade and occupied himself with more interesting things. He wrote a series of letters to the *Arkansas Gazette,* first paper to be published west of the Mississippi, telling of the injustices the Indians had suffered.

He was equally ready to defend a white man if he thought he had suffered or might suffer an injustice.

One day in Fort Smith a drunkard reeled through the streets cursing a missionary named Williams, shouting that he would beat Williams to a pulp if he could only find him. Houston stepped up to him and said:

"I am Williams. What was it you wanted with me?"

The drunkard squinted at Houston.

"Naw, you ain't Williams. Williams ain't as big as me and you're a heap bigger."

"So," said Houston, "you call me a liar. Then you must take the consequences." He drew back his fist. The drunkard scurried away.

"Naw, Mister Williams," he shouted, "I'm just plain mistaken all the way around."

## 13: "You, Sir, Are a Rascal"

NEW INDIAN AGENTS CAME TO REPLACE THOSE Jackson had removed. For a time they seemed all right but Houston soon recognized that no matter how honest the agent, sooner or later the Indians would again suffer injustice. It would continue so long as the white population moved farther and farther west, needing more and more land.

"There is no hope, Father," he told John Jolly one night.

"There is always hope," his foster father said, "if we live by our beliefs and honor our promises."

In December of 1831 the Cherokee National Council

again asked Houston to go as their ambassador to Washington with a list of grievances.

On his way Houston stopped again at Nashville and wandered over the grounds of Jackson's plantation, The Hermitage. With the broad-bladed hunting knife that he carried in his belt he cut a hickory sapling to use as a cane. He still suffered from the wounds he had received as a youth at the battle of Tohopeka. His right arm was still weak and he walked with a slight limp because of the arrow wound in his thigh.

In Washington he settled at Brown's Hotel. It was a time of much political bitterness. President Jackson's political opponents seized every occasion to criticize him. Houston remembered that on his previous visit his Indian costume had caused much comment. Borrowing money, he outfitted himself with the cutaway coat, waistcoat, tight trousers and beaver hat of an Eastern gentleman. But this did not stop Jackson's enemies from talking about him.

One of the charges was that Jackson's former secretary of war had tried by fraud to give Sam Houston a profitable contract to provide rations to the Indians in the Arkansas territory. The charge was made in the House of Representatives by Ohio Congressman William Stanbery. Although Houston had not been given the contract, Stanbery charged that he was profiting from his friendship with President Jackson.

Houston was outraged, more for Jackson's sake than for his own. He rushed to the House of Representatives determined to settle the matter with his fists. A friend persuaded him to leave. Next, he sent a note to Stanbery demanding "satisfaction," meaning either an apology or a duel. Stanbery said that he did not know Houston and would not accept the note.

"I'll introduce myself to the rascal," Houston told friends. When word of this reached Stanbery the Congressman armed himself with a pistol.

One night while strolling along Pennsylvania Avenue Houston saw Stanbery. Walking up to him, he took a flat-footed stance in front of the man and announced, "You, sir, are a rascal."

And, saying it, he began to beat the Congressman with the hickory cane he had cut back at The Hermitage. Stanbery was almost as large as Houston. One of Houston's arms was useless in a fight because of the Tohopeka wound. The Congressman should have had an advantage. But Houston was furious and Stanbery was getting the worst of it. The Congressman yanked out his pistol, aimed it at Houston's chest and pulled the trigger.

The gun clicked. It had misfired. Houston paid no attention to it. He clubbed the Congressman to the ground. Then, grabbing his victim by the feet, he yanked his legs in the air and kicked him in the back-side and flattened him on the cobblestones.

"There, you miserable puppy," said Houston. "Per-haps this will teach you care and responsibility in your public statements." And he walked away.

There was a great outcry in the House of Representa-tives the next day. Anyone who interfered with the privileges of congressmen to speak their minds in the House could be held in contempt and placed on trial. Houston was ordered to appear before the House to defend himself on the charge of contempt.

As his attorney Houston had Francis Scott Key, the man who had written "The Star-Spangled Banner." But he had little use for an attorney. For the most part he pleaded his case himself.

"Though the plowshare of ruin has driven over me and laid waste my brightest hopes," Houston declared in his speech to the House, "yet I am proud to think that under all circumstances I have endeavored to sus-tain the laws of my country and to support her institu-tions."

In defending himself Houston had an opportunity to answer all the people who had criticized his charac-ter. The case attracted wide attention, and each day the public galleries of the House were crowded with men and women who wanted to see and hear this man about whom so many strange tales were told. Men cheered him and women threw him bouquets of flowers. Once someone in the gallery shouted, "I had rather be Sam Houston in a dungeon than Stanbery on a throne."

Although public sympathy was all with Houston, the House voted him guilty of contempt and ordered the Speaker of the House to reprimand him.

The Speaker, who admired Houston as much as the crowds in the galleries, called the accused man before him and said, "It is the judgment of the House that you be reprimanded by the Speaker, and I do reprimand you accordingly."

It was a victory for Houston. Although a civil court later ordered him to pay a fine for the assault, he had spoken his mind and cleared his name. His spirits were better than they had been since he left Nashville to go into exile.

He stayed in the East a while longer, completing his business for the Cherokees. Everywhere there was talk of Texas. Adventurous men were pooling their money and setting off toward the southwest. They intended to help free Texas from Mexico. Banking firms were speculating in Texas lands, buying them at low prices and expecting them to rise sharply in value if and when Texas became free and joined the United States. Both the adventurers and the bankers talked to Houston, recognizing that he would be a valuable leader of any independence movement. Houston promised nothing to any of them. But his life-long interest in the Southwest became stronger than ever. On the long trip back he decided he would at least visit Texas. President Jackson had given him a passport of sorts and authorized him to check up on some Indian matters in Texas.

When he reached John Jolly's lodge he and his foster father sat by the fire and smoked a pipe of tobacco together.

"My father," said Houston, "you gave me the name of Colonneh, The Raven. You remember in the tales of the old men, the raven's mission was to bring fire to man. The raven tried with all his strength and spirit, and he singed himself black. But he did not succeed in bringing fire to man. Man had to find it for himself. I have tried to help my Cherokee brothers. I have not done well, but I have done the best I could. Now I go to the Mexican province of Tejas. My friends there have asked for me. They say they need me. If the Great Spirit wills it perhaps I can bring the fire to them."

John Jolly stared at the coals. Then he said, "You are right, my son. You should go among your own kind. And remember that you carry with you my heart, just as your heart will remain with us. May the Great Spirit guide you to happiness."

A few days later Houston set off riding a bobtailed

Indian pony named Jack. On the trail south he met
Elias Rector, United States Marshal for the Arkansas
Territory, and for a time they rode together. Houston
noticed the fine, strong chestnut horse that the marshal
was riding. As they traveled along he began telling
Rector what a fine pony Jack was, nimble, gentle and
hardy.

When their paths parted Houston suggested that
they trade mounts. Jack was a fine pony, but where
they were going there were many flies, and Jack had no
tail with which to switch himself. Rector good-
naturedly agreed, and Houston switched his saddle
and bed roll to the chestnut horse. He made a farewell
speech to Jack.

"You have been a good servant to me, Jack," he said.
"But there comes a time in the life of every man when
he and his friends must part. You are a faithful, sure-
footed pony, but cruel man has made you defenseless
against the common enemy of your kind—the pesky
fly. I must, therefore, part from you in pain and an-
guish."

Rector laughed. "Look, Houston," he said. "The
horse was a trade. I'd like to give you a gift as well.
The only thing I have to give is this razor. They say it's
bad luck to give a cutting tool as a gift. But I think
you've had all your bad luck. It should be good the rest
of the way."

Houston admired the razor. "I'll take it, Rector, and you have my thanks. And mark my words: Some day this razor will shave the chin of the president of a republic. You can tell your grandchildren that long after you've forgotten this fine horse I traded you out of."

The next evening Houston forded the Red River. Midstream he stopped and gazed at the red sky in the west, then continued across the river. He was in Texas.

# 14: Texas at Last

THE ROAD FROM FORT TOWSON TO NACOGDOCHES WAS not a road at all. It was barely a trail. Houston kept the rising sun on his left and the setting sun at his right and traveled steadily southward.

In all the 180 miles he saw only two people. One was a trapper, a ragged, nondescript man whose tattered clothes were pinned together with locust thorns. He gave Houston a plate of tin beans with black molasses poured over them, and warned him to watch out for "painters" on the trail. He meant panthers. He also offered the use of his cabin, but the roof was falling in. The trapper himself slept in a dugout canoe under a pile of fur robes. After trying in vain to engage the man in conversation, Houston rolled himself in a blanket and slept under a tree.

Two days later he met another man who was more talkative. He was a bee hunter, a thin little old man with bright blue eyes and long unkempt hair the color of straw. He rode a bony horse and led a pack mule, heavily laden. That night the two travelers shared a fire.

"I've been a bee hunter all my life," the old man said. "I'm not a boastful man, but I'm probably the best bee hunter alive. I can hear the bees when no one else hears a thing, and I know what they say. In summer they lead me to their trees where the honey is stored. I know their language and their habits. I've traveled all this country and know it well."

"Tell me about Texas," said Houston.

The old man seemed to ignore his question. "I know when bees will swarm and where they will go. A bee is a most curious animal."

"But I want to know about Texas," said Houston. "Are settlers from the United States still entering and settling?"

"I was coming to that," said the bee hunter. "Now a bee knows where the white man will go next and the bee goes just ahead of the white man. The Indians know that. When they see a swarm of bees in a place they'd never been seen before, the Indians know the white man will be there soon. This year there's been more swarms of bees in Texas than ever, far as I can remember. It means the white man is coming, lots of white men." He paused, and then went on: "That poor old mule of mine is loaded down with beeswax that the Mexican priests will pay me well for in San Antonio de Bexar. Makes fine candles for their missions. More bees this year than the year before, and more wax. There'll be more next year. And the year after."

"And more white men," Houston added. "Will Texas fight for her independence? Will she throw off Mexico's rule?"

"Mister, I don't know anything about men," said the bee hunter. "All I know is bees, and like I say, where the bee goes the white man follows."

Riding on toward Nacogdoches, Houston thought of what the old man had said. Mexico was trying in every way to stop the influx of settlers from the United States. She had forbidden further Anglo-American settlements near the eastern frontier. She had abolished slavery, which might have discouraged some of the immigrants from the southern states, but did not. The settlers brought their slaves along and ignored the law. Mexico had even taken to sending prison convicts into the raw state of Texas, thinking, perhaps, that the presence of the criminals would deter the new settlers. It did not.

The character of the country changed as Houston drew nearer Nacogdoches. Instead of blackjack oaks there were now tall pine and gum trees. Instead of sandy soil there was red clay, and the streams and rivers ran rusty red.

Nacogdoches was one of the oldest towns of the region. It had been a settlement of the Nacogdoche Indians long before the white men came. The Indians had left four large burial mounds out of which small white boys still dug bones and skulls and arrowheads and bits of broken pottery.

Spanish priests had established a mission there more than a century before Houston's arrival, but Nacogdoches was not a particularly religious town. It was a gateway from the southwest to the United States. It became a refuge for fugitives from justice in the United States and a headquarters for smugglers. An old stone fort in the center of the settlement, originally built for defense, was now used as a warehouse for smuggled goods.

Anglo-American settlers of Nacogdoches, both the fugitives from justice and the better class of hardworking, serious immigrants, frequently quarreled with the Mexican authorities. More than twenty years before, an American expedition from Natchez, Mississippi, had set up headquarters in the old stone fort and declared Texas independent. But a stronger Mexican force soon drove them out. Again, only six years before Houston's arrival, another American group had seized the old stone fort and declared the "Fredonian Republic" established, independent of Mexico. This rebellion too was put down.

As his weary horse plodded into Nacogdoches Houston recognized the old stone fort, and also the town's two inns. He stopped briefly at the Cantina del Monte. The tavern was dark and dingy. Mexican soldiers sat around tables, drinking and playing cards. In a corner a tremendously fat woman sat, smoking a cigar and strumming a guitar. Houston decided the atmosphere would not be restful and went on to Brown's Tavern. He tethered his horse and was shown a place on the floor where he could spread his blankets. He fell into a deep sleep.

He awoke to find someone shaking him.

"Wake up, General Sam Houston, you old Cherokee," someone was saying.

Houston rubbed his eyes and opened them.

"Sterne . . . Adolphus Sterne," he said as his eyes focused on the visitor. "What are you doing here, and how did you know I was here?"

Adolphus Sterne was a pleasant, well-educated German whom Houston had last seen in Nashville years before. Sterne had been in Texas for some time and was an important merchant and political figure in Nacogdoches. He was "alcalde" of the community, a magistrate.

Sterne laughed. "One question at a time, Sam. As for the first question, I live and do business in Nacogdoches. I am a land agent and a merchant. As for your second question, everyone in Nacogdoches and for that matter everyone in the state of Coahuila and Texas has known that you were bound to come here some day. It was only a question of when you would come."

Houston pulled on his boots, scooped cold water from a tin pail with his hands, and splashed it over his face and head. He and Sterne went into the front room of the inn and breakfasted on fried ham, hominy, and coffee made from parched corn and acorns.

"Sam," said Adolphus Sterne after the last of his ham was gone, "they say that you are coming to lead Texas in a war of independence, that you have President Jackson's blessing."

"Whoever 'they' may be," said Houston, "I'd say

'they' are making a long jump at a conclusion. It is true, as you know, that I am a friend of President Jackson's. It is true that President Jackson is interested in Texas and the Texans . . . long has been. He offered to buy the territory, as you know. It is also true that many Texans have begged me to come to Texas and give them leadership. It is also true that I am on a mission for President Jackson—a conference with the Comanche Indians at San Antonio de Bexar. It is also natural to assume that in reporting to Jackson on this mission I also will report to him on the state of Texas in general.

"But beyond that, there is nothing. I am not General Houston, nor Governor Houston, nor Congressman Houston. I am Sam Houston, private citizen, temporarily on a mission of no great importance for President Andrew Jackson. Sam Houston, private citizen and attorney at law, although sadly out of practice. If this Texas is as great and promising as everyone says, then I may become a Texan and again practice the law. That and no more, so far as I can see at the moment, Sterne."

Adolphus Sterne smiled and repeated, "So far as you can see at the moment, eh? Well, Sam, welcome to Nacogdoches. Come walk with me and you'll see many old friends here from the old days in Nashville. Some who came here because they wanted to, because they thought it was a land of opportunity; and some who came because they had to because they were in trouble, slipping away in the night and leaving a note for their families with just the initials 'G.T.T.'—'Gone to Texas.' "

Sterne and his young and pleasant Louisiana wife, Eva, insisted that Houston live with them for the remainder of his stay in Nacogdoches. The two men returned to Brown's Tavern to get Houston's horse and baggage.

"After I've rested," Houston told his host, "I shall begin the trip to San Antonio de Bexar where I am to meet the Comanches and deliver the President's message. I think I shall go by way of San Felipe de Austin. I should like to meet Stephen Austin and see his colony."

"You may catch him and you may not," said his friend. "He's a strange man, Sam. He's a man of peace who has tried to live up to his promises to the Mexican government. He's a much more patient man than most of us."

Houston was smoothing the saddle blanket on his horse.

"Patience is a great virtue, my friend, and one that I must confess I am somewhat lacking in. I think perhaps this Austin and I would make a good team."

# 15: The Conspirators

FOR CENTURIES THAT LAND NOW KNOWN AS TEXAS
was an empty spot on old Spanish maps, marked
"Tejas"—so named for the Tejas or "friendly" Indians
the Spanish first found there.

The Spanish explorers had crossed and re-crossed the
country in their endless search for gold and silver.
Spanish priests came to try to convert the Indians. A
few forts were built by soldiers and a few missions by the
priests, and a few towns grew up around the forts and
the missions. But for the most part Texas remained
unsettled until after Mexico declared her independence
of Spain in 1821.

The Mexican government, to encourage settlement of sparse country, offered grants of land to willing settlers. Stephen Austin, taking up work begun by his father, Moses Austin, was the earliest and most important of the organizers of colonies of American settlers.

Austin found many eager colonists. There had been a financial panic and times were hard in the United States. Many families were ready to try anything to better their fortunes, and the offer of free land in Texas sounded good.

There were three hundred families in Austin's original group, and they came to be known as "the old three hundred," a new aristocracy in the new land. San Felipe de Austin was the headquarters of the new colony which spread from the Lavaca to the San Jacinto River and from the Gulf northward to the Camino Real, or royal road, which ran from Nacogdoches to San Antonio de Bexar.

By the time Houston arrived in Texas there were, in the entire Austin colony, about eight thousand people, two hundred or so of them in the town of San Felipe itself. All had become Mexican citizens by accepting the Mexican land grants, although few ever considered themselves anything but United States citizens at heart.

Stephen Austin was one of the few exceptions. He was a serious and conscientious man who tried hard to live up to the duties of citizenship in his adopted country. This put him in a difficult position. His colonists frequently objected to his collecting the surveying and legal fees to which he was entitled, and considered him an agent of the Mexicans.

The Mexican government, on the other hand, regarded Austin with suspicion as an agent of the United States, the strong young country to the north, which made no secret of the fact that it would like to own Texas. Mexico was becoming alarmed at the heavy flow of newcomers from the United States. Thus Austin, trying on one hand to make the Mexicans deal justly with the colonists, and on the other trying to keep the colonists patient with the Mexican government, did not have a happy lot.

Houston had long been aware of this, had felt sympathy for Austin in his difficult role and hoped that he might visit the man in San Felipe.

After a few days' rest in Nacogdoches, Houston set out on the Atascocito Road for San Felipe de Austin. The road bore directly south, crossed the Neches River and went on to the westward to San Felipe. The road was rough and poorly marked, but it was a great improvement on the trail southward from the Red River to Nacogdoches. Occasionally Houston passed horsemen, singly or in pairs, and several times there were entire families lumbering along in a cart drawn by oxen. One night he camped with a family that had come from Kentucky. The father, two sons and their dogs had been out hunting, enjoying the new country. The woman and her daughter stayed at the oxcart, trying to wash clothes and cook food. "Mister," said the woman, "there's a saying out here that this here country's fine for men and dogs, but it's sure hard on women and oxen."

San Felipe surprised Houston with its size and tidiness. There were at least thirty houses, built of logs so carefully smoothed and joined that they appeared to be finely sawed boards. The houses were almost all alike—two rooms, each with its stone fireplace, joined by an overhead roof sheltering an open section called the "dog trot." Some of the larger houses had kitchens added at the rear. The town was neatly laid out on a high prairie overlooking a bend in the Brazos River.

As the Austin colony was made up for the most part of hard-working farmers, there was an air of industry and tidiness to the place that had been missing in Nacogdoches with all its fugitives and smugglers.

After he had gone to one of the village's two inns and thrown his bed roll on the floor beside the fireplace, where it would be warm, Houston asked the innkeeper about Austin.

"Serious Stevie, you mean," said the innkeeper, a

bulky man with a red face and large yellow mustache. "He's away. Gone to visit kinfolks. Below here on the Brazos. Probably won't be able to enjoy the visit with his kinfolks for thinking up new ways to keep us under Mexico's boot."

"You are too hard on the man," said Houston. "He had to make promises to the Mexican government."

"Promises, eh?" said the innkeeper. "If promises are so important why don't the Mexicans keep them? We might as well be in China for all the help they give us. You want to hear about them Mexicans? Hey, boy!"

A young Negro came running.

"Find Mister Jim and tell him he's got another job educating a furriner. Old Jim may be an alligator-rassling, tobacco-smuggling, slave-stealing rascal but he knows the truth about Texas and ain't afraid."

Just then Jim Bowie's broad shoulders filled the doorway.

"What's all this clapper-clawing about?" he asked.

"This here gentleman," the innkeeper began, but Bowie interrupted him. He threw both arms around Houston and pounded him on the back, in a Mexican-style greeting.

"Houston," he roared, "we've been hoping for you and looking for you, knowing that a man like you couldn't stay out of Tejas forever." He gave Texas the Spanish pronunciation, tay-hahss.

*Men who felt Texas must fight Mexico for her
independence*

"It's good to see you again, Bowie," said Houston.
"There have been some lonely and sad years since we
sat by the Mississippi and you told me of the treasure
you were going to find. Did you find it?"

"No. But I've found more important things. You are
in good time. Some of us are having a meeting tonight
and we need you there."

A few hours later Bowie led Houston through the
town's dark street. The sky was blue-black and the
stars were bright and near.

"Do you know what night it is?" Bowie asked.

Houston began counting the days of his journey, trying to calculate the date.

"It's Christmas Eve, man," said Bowie. "Maybe one
of those stars up there is the one that guided the Wise

Men, I don't know. I know naught of the stars and their courses, save the North Star. But I know that we need wise men here to counsel and guide us. Houston, I'm glad you've come, man, at last."

They stopped at a cabin door and were let in by a man who carried a rifle in the crook of his arm. A half dozen men were seated on benches by the fire. Houston recognized one of the men as William Wharton, whom he had known in Nashville. Wharton was a lawyer and plantation owner in Texas, and was known as a leader of "the war party." Unlike Stephen Austin, these men felt that Texas must fight Mexico for her independence, and the sooner the better. While Houston was with the Cherokees he had received letters from Wharton, urging him to come to Texas and help them.

Houston was admitted to the group and listened to the discussion which was full of names of people and places that were strange to him. There was talk of a fight in Velasco the previous spring in which the colonists trounced the Mexican soldiers, and of a convention that had been held in San Felipe in the fall, pressing demands on the Mexican government.

As the talk went on Houston reached in the kindling box and drew out a stick of yellow pine. With his ivory-handled clasp knife he began whittling, and a small wooden sword took shape in his hands.

There was a pause in the talk.

"General Houston," Wharton said, "I have long wanted you to come to Texas. We need a man of your stature and ability to lead us in the fight that is coming. Will you throw in your lot with us?"

Houston gazed at the wooden sword in his hand. His big fist closed on it, and the wood snapped.

"Wharton, I can give you an answer. I have certain duties to perform for President Jackson. I can assure you that the President is aware of and interested in your plight, but I can in no way pledge you his aid in your plans. As for myself, I intend to perform this mission. Then I shall settle in Texas and become a Texan, if all goes well. After that, we shall see what we shall see."

## 16: "The Finest Country"

THE NEXT NOON, CHRISTMAS DAY, HOUSTON AND Bowie ate a tremendous meal of roast goose and sweet potatoes in the kitchen of the inn, and Bowie agreed to accompany Houston to San Antonio de Bexar. Before dawn the next day they were on their way.

In San Antonio Houston was a guest in the home of Juan Martin de Veramendi, whose daughter Bowie had married. The Veramendi home was one of the largest and most distinguished in the sleepy Mexican community.

"As we say in Spanish," Bowie told him, " 'here you have your house.' I trust that here you will some day

meet my beloved wife, Ursula, our two beautiful children, and my distinguished father-in-law. They now
are in our other home in Saltillo, the capital of
Coahuila and Texas. Although Don Martin is a Mexican, and an important one, having been *alcalde* of San
Antonio and vice-governor of Coahuila and Texas,
you will find that he thinks as we do. He favors free
immigration from the United States in the interest
of developing the country, and he favors more self-
government for the settlers who come here."

Houston carefully made mental notes of this and
other conversations in San Antonio. He found his
Comanche chieftains, conveyed General Jackson's
greetings, and arranged for them to come to a meeting
in the Arkansas territory late the next spring to dis-
cuss various Indian problems with United States representatives.

Having thus completed his official business, he spent
some time longer in the Mexican town, picking up a
few words of Spanish, carefully sounding out both
Mexican and Anglo-American residents on their attitude toward the growing troubles between Texas colonists and the Mexican government.

He was particularly interested in the Alamo, a vast,
low structure of stone and adobe bricks, built more
than a century before as a mission through which the
Spanish priests hoped to civilize the Indians. Long

abandoned as a mission, it had become a garrison for Mexican troops. Walking idly around the Plaza, Houston eyed not only the Alamo but the Mexican soldiers as well. The soldiers seemed well disciplined and well equipped, but incapable of dealing with surprises.

One day while Houston watched, a lame burro came and lay down in front of a squad that was drilling. The drill leader, instead of ordering his men to do an about-face, halted them, stood and shouted and kicked at the burro, and, unable to move it, dismissed his squad. Houston's eyes squinted as he watched, and he made a mental note for future reference.

After the primitive life among the Cherokees and the rough life in the frontier towns of Nacogdoches and San Felipe, San Antonio seemed very civilized. The Veramendi mansion had a large staff of servants. In the morning a quiet servant would bring Houston a mug of steaming chocolate. At the meals there was wine, imported from Spain. In the evenings there was music and gaiety in the streets.

Houston enjoyed it and stayed as long as he felt that he could. Then he turned his horse eastward again and, following the Camino Real, rode off for Nacogdoches, and past Nacogdoches to Natchitoches, in Louisiana. Back on United States soil, he wrote to President Jackson:

To General Jackson

Dear Sir:

I am in possession of some information that doubtless will be interesting to you; and may be calculated to forward your views if you should entertain any; touching the acquisition of Texas by the United States. That such a measure is desirable by nineteen twentieths of the population of the Province, I can not doubt. They are now without laws to govern or protect them. Mexico is involved in civil war. . . .

The people of Texas are determined to form a State Government and separate from Coahuila, and unless Mexico is soon restored to order, and the Constitution revived and re-enacted, the Province of Texas will remain separate from the confederacy of Mexico. She has already beaten and expelled all the troops of Mexico from her soil, nor will she permit them to return. She can defend herself against the whole power of Mexico, for really Mexico is powerless and penniless, to all intents and purposes. Her want of money taken in connection with the course which Texas *must and will adopt,* will render a transfer of

Texas inevitable to some power, and if the United States does not press for it, England will most assuredly obtain it by some means. . . .

I have traveled near five hundred miles across Texas, and am now enabled to judge pretty correctly of the soil, and the resources of the country, and I have no hesitancy in pronouncing it the finest country to its extent upon the globe. There can be no doubt but that the country . . . would sustain a population of ten millions of souls. . . . It is probable that I may make Texas my abiding place! In adopting this course I will never forget the Country of my birth. . . .

Sam Houston

With a soft piece of leather Houston cleaned the eagle quill with which he had written the letter, and read back through it slowly, smiling to himself as he read.

"Texas," he said softly as he folded the letter into an envelope. "Texas. . . ."

## *17:* *"Volunteers Are Invited"*

Having completed his mission for president Jackson, Houston decided to return to Nacogdoches and re-establish himself as a lawyer.

He made his home with Adolphus Sterne and his wife. The Sternes' home was pleasant. Eva Sterne was a cultured and educated woman. In the evenings Houston and Adolphus Sterne would sit sipping strong black French coffee while Eva Sterne softly played the spinet piano.

"Any raw, new province such as this," Sterne said one night, "will attract the roughest, wildest element from the more civilized places." As he spoke they could

hear the sounds of a street fight outside, a nightly oc-
currence in Nacogdoches. He continued, "It will also
bring honest settlers, but the wild ones make more
noise. They demand, always, rash, headstrong meas-
ures. They are the first to start a fight, the first to flee.
Texas has more than her share of such men."

"Yet," Houston said, "such men, given the proper
leadership, leadership that is strong in courage, wise
in counsel and cool in an emergency, can be made to
work wonders—wonders such as the freedom of Texas."

Sterne smiled wisely at Houston.

"Do not mistake my meaning," Houston added hast-
ily. "My own intentions are simple. I intend to practice
law, nothing more. That and execute the responsibilities of citizenship in my new community."

Sterne continued to smile, but said nothing. He had
quietly persuaded some of his influential fellow-
townsmen to name Houston a delegate to another convention being held at San Felipe de Austin.

The convention's tone was optimistic. Antonio Lopez
de Santa Anna was stepping into the Mexican presidency. It was thought that Santa Anna would be more
friendly to the Texas colonists than recent govern-
ments had been. The San Felipe convention was called
for the same day that Santa Anna was to take office.

Houston was the tallest man in the group. Around

his shoulders he now wore, instead of an Indian blanket, a brightly colored Mexican *serape*.

The other delegates, Stephen Austin among them, were anxious to meet him. Austin was a pale, slender man with a nervous air. Establishing and operating the colony and trying to keep peace between the colonists and Mexico had been hard on him.

"It is a pleasure to have you with us, General Houston," he told the newcomer. "Texas needs such men as you."

Houston thanked Austin gravely. He liked the man. And as the convention got under way he was glad to see that "the war party," led by his old friend William Wharton, had become more moderate and less unfriendly toward Austin.

The convention adopted a politely worded request for statehood, separation from the state of Coahuila and recognition as a state with a government of its own. It also adopted a proposed state constitution which Houston drafted, copying it after that of Tennessee.

It was decided that Stephen Austin should take the convention's resolutions to Mexico City. Since he had remained stubbornly loyal to his adopted government he probably would be given a friendly audience by the new Mexican president.

Before Austin left San Felipe for the long journey to

the Mexican capital, Houston shook his hand and wished him well.

"And believe me," he added, as they parted, "Sam Houston will do nothing to embarrass you or prejudice in any way the mission which you are undertaking. Houston's warmest wishes go with you."

For a time there was peace in the Texas colonies. Houston practiced law in Nacogdoches and became widely known among all classes—the serious, hard-working settlers, the fugitives, the soldiers of fortune, the hunters, smugglers, operators of mule caravans and dealers in wild horses.

Then word came back from Mexico: Stephen Austin had been put in prison by the Mexican government! The Mexican authorities at first listened to his pleas for Texas, indicated they were sympathetic and allowed him to start on the long trip home. But before he reached Texas orders were issued for his arrest on a charge of treason. He was accused of stirring up rebellion in the Texas colony. He was hauled back to Mexico City and thrown in a dungeon.

Again feeling ran high among the American colonists in Texas. Individuals and groups of men came to Houston, asking that he take leadership in a war of independence. Houston's answer was always the same: Wait.

"We must not," he said, again and again, "plunge

Texas into a bloody struggle with Mexico before we are prepared for it."

Stephen Austin finally was released by the Mexican government and arrived back in Texas in the early autumn of 1835. He was a changed man. He had reached a painful decision: that there was little hope of a peaceful settlement of the Texas question, that if Texas was to be a separate state she must fight for it.

Word of Austin's attitude ran through the settlements, and preparations were made for another meeting at San Felipe.

Back in Nacogdoches, fellow citizens elected Houston a delegate to the new meeting, and also named him "Commander in chief of troops of the department of Nacogdoches."

There were no troops, but Houston sent off to New Orleans for a general's uniform and with his eagle-quill pen wrote out a proclamation: "Volunteers are invited to our standard. Liberal bounties of land will be given to all who will join our ranks with a good rifle and one hundred rounds of ammunition. . . . The morning of glory is dawning upon us."

Later the new convention at San Felipe elected Houston commander in chief of all Texas forces.

There were, by this time, Texas forces in the field. In a series of impromptu engagements they had begun the chain of events that was to lead to war.

# 18: Santa Anna Moves

THE FIRST SHOTS OF THE TEXAS REVOLUTION WERE fired at the town of Gonzales. The Mexicans had sent a detachment of soldiers to Gonzales to reclaim a cannon they had given the colonists earlier to protect themselves against the Indians. The colonists buried the cannon in a peach orchard and made themselves a flag with the defiant slogan "Come and get it!" When volunteers from nearby towns arrived they dug up the cannon, loaded it with nails, bolts and scrap iron, and fired it just once at the menacing Mexicans. One Mexican was killed and the rest retreated.

A few days later another group of volunteers attacked the Mexican arms depot at Goliad, overcame the Mexican guards and seized three hundred muskets, two cannon and a good supply of ammunition for both.

Volunteers from both Gonzales and Goliad marched on toward San Antonio de Bexar where still others were preparing to lay siege to the Mexican garrison commanded by Santa Anna's brother-in-law, General Cos.

After a series of skirmishes outside San Antonio, Ben Milam, a veteran plainsman who had joined the volunteers, decided the time had come to take the town by storm. He waved his rifle and shouted, "Who'll go into Bexar with old Ben Milam?" It was December 4, 1835. Three hundred men rallied around him and stormed into San Antonio. Cannon fire rattled in the narrow streets, rifle balls whistled in the air and battering rams thundered against the adobe and stone walls where the Mexicans had hidden. Milam was killed, but after five days of fierce fighting General Cos and his fourteen hundred men surrendered. They were sent on their way, pledged to get out of Texas.

The series of successes fanned feeling among the Texans. Men with rifles swarmed to join the victorious force at San Antonio. Francis Johnson and James Grant assumed leadership of the forces and began talking of an invasion of Matamoros, the Mexican town on the Rio Grande. They moved southward to Refugio, near the Gulf.

Although Houston was commander in chief of the Texas forces he had little to do with these victories. He had in fact expressed doubt that San Antonio could be taken without artillery. After the San Antonio victory he had tried to control the bounding optimism of other leaders. While inspired groups of volunteers may achieve brilliant first victories, he warned, it is the well-trained, disciplined army that wins a war in the long run.

Flushed with victory, the Texans paid little heed to their commander in chief. Houston joined the volunteer forces at Refugio and tried to dissuade them from the Matamoros expedition which would, he was certain, result in failure. He was laughed at.

Houston tried to advise Francis Johnson, one of the leaders, against the foolhardy project.

"You should know this Matamoros expedition is folly," Houston told him. "You have been a soldier and have served under fire. You know what happens when you fight with little hope of reinforcement. If you win immediately, all is well. But if you suffer a reverse, you are done for."

"Yes," Johnson countered, "but these Mexicans cannot fight. We have seen that at Gonzales and at Goliad and in San Antonio. We will march into Matamoros and take it—and all the riches to be had there. That is all. With a bounty of land and the spoils of this campaign I'll have what I came west for—a fortune."

"You are making a grievous mistake," Houston replied. "The victories we have had over the Mexicans have been over poorly organized forces that were not prepared for real resistance. What happened at San Antonio was an insult to the Mexican government. If what I hear of Santa Anna is true he will not let it go unavenged. And this time the Mexicans will come prepared for trouble."

While Houston was in Refugio, the temporary government that had been set up at San Felipe relieved him of his responsibilities as commander in chief. He was still a general, but without a command.

Unable to convince the volunteers that the Matamoros project was hopeless, Houston left Refugio and rode sadly back to San Felipe. He requested and received a furlough until March first, when there was to be another convention at Washington-on-the-Brazos.

Then, once more, as he had done so often in the past,

119

he prepared to go off among the Indians. He shed his military uniform, put on buckskins, and wound an Indian blanket around his shoulders to shield him from the winter wind.

George Washington Hockley, a younger man whom he had known first in Washington, later in Nashville and finally in Nacogdoches, watched him.

"Where are you going, Sam?"

"To see my friends, the Cherokees."

"To stay?" Hockley's tone was worried. He knew how Houston had exiled himself among the Indians in the past.

Houston laughed. "No. Not to stay. I want only to make certain that the Indians in Texas will not fight against us in the war that is coming as surely as daylight follows dawn. I'll be back, George, in time for the Washington convention."

He paused. "And if it is any comfort to you, George, I intend to see Texas a free nation, despite the high-minded but misguided efforts of our pudding-headed Sunday soldiers and fair-weather patriots."

He rode away.

Meanwhile, far to the south in the deserts of Coahuila, a short, sad-faced little man in a dress uniform rode at the head of a column of three thousand Mexican troops, moving north at top speed through the burning days and freezing nights. Their tramping feet raised clouds of dust in the bright winter sunlight. It was Antonio Lopez de Santa Anna, the Mexican dictator, who called himself the "Napoleon of the West." A supremely egotistical and heartless little man, he was bound for San Antonio de Bexar, determined to wipe out in blood the insult that the upstart Americans had flung at Mexico.

# 19: Death at the Alamo

THE TOWN OF WASHINGTON-ON-THE-BRAZOS WAS A much simpler town than its fancy name implied. It was a miserable settlement, even by frontier standards. Texans called it simply Washington.

Laid out in a woods on the edge of the muddy Brazos River, its main thoroughfare was still full of stumps. In the last days of February a driving rain made the road a quagmire. There were about a dozen cabins, some finished, some unfinished.

The temporary government that had been set up at San Felipe had gone to pieces, torn by jealousy and indecision. The convention at Washington, called for

March 1, 1836, was to try to replace it with something more durable.

As delegates began arriving in the last days of February, there was a scramble to find places to sleep. Early arrivals found places in the crude cabins. Some lucky ones slept in the sweet-smelling wood shavings on the floor of a carpenter's shop. Others slept in the open, under the dripping trees.

But worse than the physical discomfort was the disheartening news. Santa Anna had at least six thousand men in the field, pledged to exterminate the rebellious Texans. His force was divided into three well-organized and highly disciplined commands. What did the Texans have to meet them?

They had a hundred-odd men at the Alamo in San Antonio under Jim Bowie and William Barret Travis. Houston had urged them in vain to blow up their fortifications and retreat to a more defensible position.

They had another hundred-odd at San Patricio under Johnson and Grant, the men who had talked glowingly of invading Matamoros and making their men rich with Mexican spoils.

They had less than five hundred under Fannin at Goliad. There were a few other bands of volunteers, drifting aimlessly. The largest group was at Gonzales.

Over-confidence, confusion and refusal to accept a

central command had wrecked the once-promising revolutionary army. Houston, whose command they had not accepted, was off somewhere talking with the Indians.

On February 28th a courier, his clothes soaked with mud and rain, rode his horse into the center of Washington where the delegates were gathered and handed them a message. It was from Travis at the Alamo:

> To the People of Texas & All Americans in the World:
>
> . . . am besieged by a thousand or more of the Mexicans under Santa Anna, I have sustained a continual bombardment and cannonade for 24 hours & have not lost a man. The enemy has demanded a surrender at discretion, otherwise, the garrison are to be put to the sword . . . if the fort is taken—I have answered the demand with a cannon shot & our flag still waves proudly from the wall. *I shall never surrender or retreat.* Then, I call on you in the name of Liberty, of patriotism & everything dear to the American character, to come to our aid with all dispatch. The enemy is receiving reinforcements daily & will no doubt increase to three or four thousand in four or five days. If this is

neglected, I am determined to sustain myself
as long as possible.

The delegates read the message. Some groaned, but
most of them remained silent. An unfinished house
with cotton cloth nailed over the open windows and
door frames was their meeting place. The wet wind bil-
lowed the damp cloth and the candles flickered.

The convention could not begin until all the delegates were there. But one delegate was more important
than the rest. Where was Houston? When was he coming?

The next day Houston rode into Washington, his
mud-spattered Indian blanket wrapped tightly about
him. A few of the delegates met him in the street,
raised their hats in the air and cheered.

"We've got to march to the Alamo and help them
boys, General," shouted one of the men in the street.
" 'Stead of sittin' here doin' nothin'."

"Yes, sir, let's go! Will you lead us, General?"
shouted another.

Houston held up a hand.

"Just a minute," he said, his deep voice calm. "What
is all this about?"

They told him of Travis' message.

Houston listened quietly. Then he said:

"We've made the mistake once, men, of flying off to

125

do we know not what, just to be doing something. Let us not make that mistake again. Let us first do what is expected of us here, let us determine our course. Then let us find the best way to follow that course."

The delegates settled down to business. A committee drew up a declaration of independence. One by one the delegates signed it. Their hands were shaking with the cold, for a "norther" had driven the temperature down to thirty-three degrees. Houston's signature was larger and bolder than the rest. Independence Day, March 2nd, was also his birthday, his forty-third.

For the second time, Houston was chosen commander in chief of the Texas forces, or what was left of them. Then came a second message from Travis at the Alamo. It was read to the delegates:

> The spirits of my men are still high, although they have had much to depress them. We have contended for ten days against an enemy whose numbers are variously estimated from fifteen hundred to six thousand men . . . I hope your honorable body will hasten on reinforcements . . . our supply of ammunition is limited.

Excitement ran through the delegates like a wave. One of them jumped to his feet and shouted a pro-

*All the defenders of the Alamo were killed*

posal that the delegates adjourn, arm themselves, and march to relieve Travis and his men.

Houston, still calm, reminded them that the important business of the delegates was to form a government so that past disasters would not be repeated. Meanwhile he would go at once to try to reorganize whatever Texas forces there were in the field. He would dispose his forces between the Mexicans and the meeting in Washington so that the convention could continue uninterrupted.

These forces, when Houston left Washington to take command in the field, consisted of Houston himself, three recent volunteers, and George Hockley, whom Houston appointed as his aide. They headed for Gonzales where, according to reports, there was a sizeable group of volunteers.

En route, Houston dismounted from his horse and placed his ear on the ground, Indian fashion. If cannon had still been firing at the Alamo, more than a hundred miles to the west, he could have heard the vibrations in the earth. He heard nothing. "We'll never again hear from Travis," he told Hockley.

Travel was slow, and it took Houston and his companions five days to reach Gonzales. Houston found three hundred seventy-five volunteers camped beside the Guadalupe River. They were for the most part inexperienced. They were short on rations although

Houston noted with pleasure that they did have two cannons in working condition. Without pausing for food or rest, he formed the volunteers into companies, appointed commanders and began drilling the men.

While he was still giving orders a group of townspeople from Gonzales approached, leading two tattered Mexicans. Women in the group were crying bitterly. A spokesman explained: The two had just arrived from San Antonio and brought word that the Alamo had fallen the previous Sunday and that all its defenders had been killed.

"Arrest those men," Houston shouted to Hockley. "They are spies, sent to spread fear among us with lies."

He saw that his quick words had comforted the townspeople. But in his heart he knew that what the Mexicans said was true. The truth at this point might throw both the town and his raw volunteers into a state of panic. A few days' delay might give him time to organize them.

Late that night, sick at heart over the tragedy of the Alamo which he knew could have been avoided, he sat by candlelight and composed a dispatch to Fannin at Goliad. Burn the town, he ordered, so that when the enemy comes it will give him no shelter. Blow up all fortifications; disperse the people; sink your cannon in the river and retreat with all haste to Victoria.

The next day more disheartening news arrived. The ill-advised expeditionary forces which Grant and Johnson had hoped to lead against Matamoros had been wiped out at San Patricio and Agua Dulce. Houston took no comfort from the fact that he had tried to stop the reckless expedition of the brave but misguided men.

# 20: *The Runaway Scrape*

THE NEXT DAY WAS SUNDAY, BUT THERE WAS NO
Sabbath rest on the banks of the Guadalupe at
Gonzales. Drill sergeants put the volunteers through
their paces. Houston and Hockley conferred with the
officers. Clerks canvassed available equipment and supplies.

At noon "Deaf" Smith rode into camp. A well-
known frontier scout, Erastus Smith was to become one
of the most valuable men in Houston's forces. He was
hard of hearing, and throughout the frontier country he
was nicknamed "Deaf," pronounced "deef." With him
Deaf Smith brought a pale young woman whose clothes

were stained with blood. Her name was Mrs. Almaron Dickerson. Her husband, a lieutenant, was one of those killed at the Alamo. She verified the tale the Mexicans had brought earlier. She had been in the Alamo but was freed by the Mexicans. The men who were not killed in the fighting were ordered killed by Santa Anna after the Alamo fell.

Before the end came Travis had taken his sword and drawn a line on the dirt floor. Those who wanted to leave could do so while there was still a chance. Those who wanted to stay were invited to step over the line. All the men stepped across. Jim Bowie, severely ill, asked comrades to carry his cot to Travis' side of the line.

Afterwards, the bodies were stacked like kindling in the plaza before the Alamo, with alternate layers of wood, and burned. There was not a single survivor of the one hundred seventy-four men who had defended the fortress.

Houston sighed as he heard the story. He knew what the effect would be among his troops and the towns-people of Gonzales. He issued orders for evacuation of the town and a general retreat. Carts were reserved for women and children. Heavy equipment was to be dumped in the river; they would take only what the men could carry on their backs. By nightfall the column was under way and the town of Gonzales was in flames.

Rumors had spread like wildfire. One was that Santa Anna was marching toward them and would soon attack them. Several dozen volunteers deserted and fled eastward, spreading panic as they went. It was the beginning of what Texans later called "The Runaway Scrape."

Houston's marching column moved slowly, hampered by refugees whom the General refused to leave behind. On one occasion he held up the column while a scouting party went back thirty miles to pick up a blind woman and her six children, who had been left behind. Her husband had died at the Alamo.

The deserters had done their work, spreading fear and panic. The countryside was empty. In houses there were partially eaten meals on the table. Hungry chickens ran after Houston's troops, flapping their wings for food. Cows bellowed to be milked. Along the road were oxcarts, left by settlers who decided they could move faster on foot.

As they marched along a courier caught up with Houston and gave him a message from Fannin at Goliad: Fannin refused to obey Houston's order to retreat. Houston shook his head, turned to Hockley and said:

"This, Hockley," pointing to the marching column, "is the last hope of Texas."

He tried to keep up the good spirits of his bedraggled troops. He would ride along the column, counting aloud. Then he would announce to the troops how strong they were, always exaggerating their numbers. It lifted the men's spirits.

When they reached the Colorado the river's banks were lined with civilian refugees trying to get across. Houston assured them they would all move before his troops crossed.

Finally, all were safely on the east side. In short order a Mexican force under General Sesma moved up on the west side, and soldiers of the two armies stared at one another across the quick-flowing river.

Hotheads among the volunteers wanted to attack the forces across the river. It was not a large group. Houston counseled patience.

Then a courier arrived bringing word that Fannin and all his men, after a bitter fight at Goliad, had surrendered, as Houston knew they must. Again the hotheads demanded an attack on the Mexicans across the river to avenge the loss at Goliad. Houston refused; he knew that Sesma was waiting for reinforcements which might arrive at any time. His own group of soldiers was all that Texas had. He could not risk them.

And that night Sesma's force was heavily reinforced.

The next evening Houston issued orders for a quiet retreat, leaving campfires burning so the enemy would not know of their departure.

Hockley alone knew how his chief had been saddened by the defeats and the loss of lives the Texans had suffered. But Houston never let the volunteers guess this. During the day he rode or walked beside the men, talking to them, telling them tales. He never seemed to rest or eat. Occasionally he would throw a few grains of corn in his mouth and chew them.

At four o'clock in the morning he would give three taps on a drum as a signal to rise. There was no bugler to blow tattoo or reveille.

During the night hours he would sit and talk with Hockley or, by himself, prowl the outposts of the camp. Once when he found a sentry sleeping at his post he ordered the man shot. The man was not shot, but the order had its effect. Discipline became much tighter.

The raggle-taggle force reached the Brazos River and moved southward along its west bank. Word reached them that Fannin and his men, after surrendering, had been cold-bloodedly massacred by the Mexicans, just as had the survivors of the Alamo.

Feeling ran high in Houston's marching column. Again the hotheads, impatient with the constant retreat, talked of mutiny, of electing another commander from among themselves. Houston stared them down.

When they came to the Groce plantation Houston called a halt of his grumbling, footsore crew. The army had grown with volunteers picked up along the way, and shrunk as various ones deserted. Now there were about five hundred.

The Groce plantation was one of the earliest and finest in Texas. Jared Groce had come out to Texas fifteen years before from Alabama with a caravan of wagons, furniture, farm implements and seed, and had built a fine home of hand-polished logs on a high bluff over the Brazos. Houston had never been here before, but when he was in the Cherokee nation he had received one letter from his old friend William Wharton, written from the Groce plantation. The letter urged Houston to come and lead the Texans to independence. Wharton was Jared Groce's son-in-law.

Houston told this to Hockley as they stood admiring the fine house with its view of the river.

"And I'm afraid the Houston that finally arrived, Hockley, is not quite the conquering hero they had in mind," Houston said, rubbing his whiskers with a dirt-caked hand and gazing down at his torn buckskin clothing.

After seeing to it that a temporary camp was laid out for his men, and ordering two beef carcasses roasted to feed them, Houston took a bath in a tin tub and wrote to the new secretary of war of the Republic of Texas, Thomas Jefferson Rusk.

"I hope I can keep them together," he wrote, referring to his demoralized and rebellious crew. "I have thus far succeeded beyond my hopes. I will do the best I can, but, be assured, the fame of Jackson could never compensate me for my anxiety and mental pain."

David Burnet, the president of the newly declared republic, sided with those who were impatient with Houston's delays. Burnet, a tense little man, and his government had fled from Washington-on-the-Brazos, despite Houston's urging that they stay there. The government's flight caused even more panic among the settlements. Now Burnet was at Harrisburg. He wrote Houston a curt note:

> Sir: The enemy are laughing you to scorn.
> You must fight.

Houston angrily thrust the dispatch in his pocket and went about his business. In the camp he ordered two graves dug and posted notices that they would be filled with mutineers.

But, without knowing it, Houston had reached and passed the lowest point of his military fortunes. The grumblers still grumbled, but there were fewer of them. The Groce family put at Houston's disposal an unlimited supply of beef and corn, and his men were well fed for a change. Women of the Groce family had medicines and bandages for those who were ill or injured. The rain fell incessantly and the river rose, but the spirit and morale of the troops were improving.

More volunteers came into camp. So did two six-pound cannons donated by citizens of Cincinnati, Ohio. Artillerymen went to work salvaging metals to convert into ammunition—old pipe, horseshoes, plowshares, even a sack of Mexican silver coins the Groces had been paid for a shipment of cotton.

A small steamer, the *Yellowstone,* was tied at Groce's landing, loading cotton from last year's crop. Houston negotiated with the skipper to carry his men and equipment across the rain-swollen Brazos. The skipper agreed, and on April 13th, after a fortnight's rest, Houston's troops were on the road again. With their bodies rested, and their spirits high, their discipline was better than it had ever been before.

While this had been going on, Santa Anna, the Napoleon of the West, had been indulging himself in some of history's greatest military miscalculations.

The sad-faced little commander, reviewing in his mind the bloody victories at San Patricio, Agua Dulce, the Alamo and Goliad, concluded that all surviving Texans were in retreat. He split up his forces into task

*Houston gave the order to march to the right*

forces and sent them out after the fleeing Texans like so many hounds after rabbits.

On March 31st, the day that Houston reached Groce's landing, Santa Anna set out in leisurely fashion from San Antonio. He traveled in style. He and his staff, smartly uniformed, rode at the head of the column of foot soldiers and cavalry, all uniformed and well equipped.

When he reached the still-smoking ruins of San Felipe which Houston's forces had fired during their retreat, Santa Anna realized that Houston still had a force of some sort encamped down the Brazos. He considered attacking them there, but deciding that it was a minor matter which could be handled at any time, he marched his men toward Harrisburg, to the southeast. There he hoped to catch and capture the fugitive Texas government.

Santa Anna calmly proceeded to Harrisburg. The town was deserted. The government had moved on to Galveston Island in the Gulf of Mexico. Santa Anna moved on to Morgan's Point, looking out across Galveston Bay. The hound had his rabbit in the log. All he had to do was wait. The fact that four other large detachments of his army were scattered widely over the face of the new Republic of Texas did not bother him. Not the Napoleon of the West.

Houston, through Deaf Smith and other scouts, had kept close track of the Mexicans' movements, and there was general knowledge among his troops that Santa Anna had gone toward Harrisburg.

Now, as they moved out along the road east from Groce's plantation, Houston's men talked quietly among themselves. Not far ahead there was a fork in the trail. One branch led to the enemy. The other went eastward toward the United States frontier. Some thought Houston intended to retreat all the way to the frontier in the hope of getting the United States to intervene.

Even Hockley was puzzled. Close as they were, Houston had not confided his plans to him.

As they neared the fork in the road Houston halted

the column. Deaf Smith appeared ahead of the column, riding toward them. He approached Houston, leaned over and spoke softly in his ear. Houston asked a question. Deaf Smith cupped his ear to listen, then nodded his head.

Houston turned and gave the order to march—to the right—toward Harrisburg. The tall gaunt man stood watching as his men marched by. Some were grinning, some laughing. They were happy.

The retreat was ended. They were marching to attack.

# 21: *"Victory or Death"*

THE ROUTE TOWARD HARRISBURG LAY OVER A LOW,
flat prairie. The grass was high and the ground was
soft with the spring rains. Time and again the wagons
and gun carriages would sink to the hubs in the cling-
ing mud. When this happened Houston would dis-
mount, strip off his buckskin jacket, and help the men
unload and unhitch the wagons and carry them past the
mudholes. The "Twin Sisters," as the cannons were
called, had to be dismounted from their carriages and
rolled and slid across the mud until firm ground was
reached.

The first night on the prairie they slept on the open

142

ground in the driving rain. In Houston's entire force there was not a single tent.

A Negro who had been captured by the Mexicans and later released, joined the column and sought out Houston. "Mister Santa Anna," he reported, "said to tell Mister Houston that he knows where he is, up there in them bushes, and as soon as his crew whips them land thieves down there, he'll come up and smoke him out."

Houston smiled and shrugged.

On April 18th the column was opposite Harrisburg, or what had been Harrisburg. It had been burned to the ground. The troops were tired. They had marched more than fifty miles in little more than two days under difficult conditions.

Deaf Smith swam across Buffalo Bayou, which separated the troops from the ruins of Harrisburg, and returned with two prisoners. One of the Mexicans was a courier, and in his large buckskin wallet was a dispatch. It revealed that Santa Anna's army, under the command of Santa Anna himself, was still in the trap formed by Buffalo Bayou on the north, the San Jacinto River on the east, and Galveston Bay on the south.

Houston was elated.

"We've got our monkey up a tree," he told Hockley. "With this we may end the war." Then he ordered the men to close ranks and he spoke to them:

"If there are any here," he said, "who shrink from the issue, they need not cross the bayou. Some must perish, but it will be glorious to fall in such a cause. Remember the Alamo. Remember Goliad. Victory or death. There will be no defeat. Victory is as certain as God reigns. Trust in the God of the just, and fear not."

The troops took up Houston's words and shouted them back: "Remember the Alamo! Victory or death!"

Awed by the occasion, a young Tennessean told the man next to him, "I feel like I'm a-standing on the drop-edge of yonder. It's sort of holy."

The troops marched a little farther east along the north bank of the bayou. A leaky old boat was found, and a cable of horsehair ropes, tied together, was rigged so that the boat could be pulled back and forth without drifting downstream.

Houston himself went across in the first boatload, swimming his horse beside the boat.

Thomas Jefferson Rusk, the minister of war, had joined Houston's forces on the Brazos. He was not an experienced soldier but he was a trustworthy man, and Houston left him in command on the north bank of the bayou while the troops were ferried across, a boatload at a time. If the Mexicans had attacked they would have found the small Texas force divided.

Finally they were all across, and the column moved slowly forward. Orders were passed back down the

144

line in whispers, from man to man. Wheels were muffled in rags and the men moved eastward with all caution. At their left, bordering Buffalo Bayou, were groves of oaks that afforded cover. On their right was prairie, and off to the south, beyond the prairie, lay Santa Anna and his army.

They crossed a narrow wooden bridge over Vince's Bayou, and nothing but the prairie separated them from the enemy.

"From here there is no escape," Houston whispered to Hockley.

Night fell, and the force inched slowly along the bayou. Just before dawn Houston halted the column. They were near the junction of Buffalo Bayou with the San Jacinto River. He disposed the men among the thick oak groves and told them they might light small cook-fires for breakfast.

"Ah'm so hungry," drawled a boy from North Carolina, "ah could eat a bull and it a-bellerin'."

Some of the men found a few cows in the bottomland next to the bayou, quickly cut their throats and soon had beefsteaks grilling on green sticks over the small fires.

But the men had no time to eat their breakfasts. Over the prairie from the south came the clear notes of a bugle. Houston ordered his men to arms, still under cover of the woods. The twin six-pound cannons were

*One of Houston's subordinate officers let his men get*

wheeled into position at the edge of the woods, pointing south over the prairie.

"This is not a full-scale attack," Houston told Hockley. "He is probing our position to see if his way is clear to the ferry across the San Jacinto. He will want to move on to the east, but first he wants to test our strength."

A line of skirmishers came in view across the prairie. Behind them were two columns, one of infantry, one of cavalry. Between them was the artillery, a single cannon, a large, brass twelve-pounder.

*involved in a running fight with the Mexicans*

Houston mounted his big white stallion and rode along the front of his line, calming his men and cautioning them against firing too soon. But the Twin Sisters were primed and ready to be fired for the first time. There had never been enough spare powder to fire them in practice.

Houston gave a signal, and the first of his cannons roared. It was well aimed. Several Mexican horses went down, and the Mexican cannon gave a lurch; its carriage had been hit. The Mexicans managed to fire it anyway, but its aim was off, and the charge whistled harmlessly through the new green oak leaves, showering down twigs.

The Mexican skirmishers began firing. A rifle ball struck Houston's bridle, and another one hit Joe Neill, the artillery officer, in the leg. When Houston gave the signal the Texas riflemen, each with a fixed target, fired a volley and the line of Mexican skirmishers wilted. Santa Anna decided to withdraw. He had tested the temper of the Texans.

Younger officers begged Houston to let them pursue the Mexicans. Houston, who had had trouble with subordinate officers since the first of the campaign, ignored them. One of them, on a reconnoitering trip to the Mexican lines which Houston had authorized, let his cavalrymen get involved in a running fight. To Houston it was apparent that the younger man was trying to involve the Texans in a major engagement before they were ready for it.

That night there was no effort at silence or secrecy. The Texans and the Mexicans knew each other's location. Scouts from both sides watched the enemy during the night to detect any move.

The Texans had bright fires blazing. Slabs of beef were roasting over the fires, and dough was baking on sticks in the coals. Men cleaned and oiled their rifles, replacing the old charges with new, and ground their bowie knives on the stones until the edges were razor-sharp. The broad-bladed knives which Jim Bowie had introduced to Texas had been honored with his name.

The sky was clear and dark and the stars were bright. The ground was dry under the trees and there was opportunity for sound sleep. But few slept soundly. The men were sure they would attack at dawn. They lay on the ground beside their rifles and stared at the coals of the fires, but few slept.

General Houston was an exception. With his head on a coil of artillery rope that had been used to pull the cannons through the mud, he retired early for the first time in weeks, and slept soundly.

## 22: *"Remember the Alamo!"*

AT 4:00 A.M. CAME THE USUAL THREE TAPS ON THE
drum to arouse the troops. Every morning since
Gonzales the General himself had given the three
taps on the drum to awaken his men. Then, having
been up all night, he would lie down for a few hours'
sleep until daylight and time to march.

This time the drumbeats did not sound quite the
same. The General was sound asleep and for the first
time someone else beat the drum.

There were no groans, no complaints about aching
backs. All the men were ready for the attack they were
sure would start at daybreak. Still the General slept.

150

First light came, and then broad day. Finally the General, his face in the glare of the bright sun, awoke. He had slept straight through the night. He gazed at the sky and said, half aloud, "The sun of Austerlitz has arisen again." It was at Austerlitz that Napoleon defeated the combined armies of Russia and Austria, one of the greatest military victories of all time.

Then the General walked to the edge of Buffalo Bayou, washed himself and put a clean bandage on the still unhealed shoulder wound he had received at the battle of Tohopeka.

He walked slowly back to the camp. Soldiers looked at him questioningly. Houston greeted them, smiled and said nothing. Seating himself on the same coil of rope on which he had slept, he ate a few grains of dry corn, and stared at a crudely drawn map of the terrain. With a forefinger he traced lines on the map.

A shout went down the line. Soldiers were pointing off across the prairie. There was a column of gray-clad marching men, coming from the west and headed for Santa Anna's camp. There were perhaps three or four hundred in the column.

"More Mexicans," the men shouted. "Santy Anny's getting reinforced!"

Houston held up a hand.

"Don't let yourselves be fooled by an old Mexican trick, men," he said, his voice steady. "Those are the same men they had yesterday. They've marched them out and marched them back again to make us think they are being reinforced. Calm yourselves. We'll take them in good time."

He called Deaf Smith to him again. Smith nodded and disappeared over the prairie toward the Mexicans. An hour later he was back, shouting:

"It's just as the General said. It's all humbug. Them's the same Mexicans we saw yesterday!"

Later, however, he came up to Houston and whispered:

"It's like you thought, General. Those are reinforcements. Three hundred and fifty men under General Cos. Made a forced march from Brazos after hearing the cannons yesterday."

Houston nodded. "We can't take a chance on any more reinforcements, Smith." He pointed to two sharp axes that he had ordered earlier from the puzzled quartermaster. "Take those axes and some help. Go cut and burn the bridge over Vince's Bayou. That's the only entrance to our battleground. It is also our only exit. Our boys will learn that 'Victory or death' is something more than a brave motto."

Smith bobbed his head. "This looks a good deal like a fight, General," he said.

"Come back like eagles, Smith, or you will be late

for the day." Houston slapped Smith on the back and the scout left.

In the camp under the oak trees there was an uneasy quiet. Men would peer out across the plain to where the Mexicans lay. They talked in low voices. Some were impatient; others nervous. All of them now and again looked at the General for some indication of what was to come next.

There was much grumbling in the camp, particularly among officers. Many of them felt that Houston was letting opportunity go begging. Houston called them into a council of war and let them argue the matter out. This officer advanced one plan, this one another, a third a completely different procedure. Houston did not say a word. When the officers had embroiled themselves in a hopelessly tangled argument, Houston walked away and left them.

Hockley approached him. His face was distressed.

"Why don't you tell them your plan, General?" he asked. "You could stop all this quarreling."

"Hockley, I've kept my own counsel from the start, and I keep it now. I grant you we could have attacked earlier and probably we would have won. Probably. But we would have done it with heavy losses. When I attack I will win and I will win without losing a dozen men. I retreated from Guadalupe to the Brazos and advanced from the Brazos to the San Jacinto without losing a man or an animal. The stakes are too great, Hockley, and our forces too small, for me to take any chances. If I took a needless risk with our few men, merely for the sake of a pleasant atmosphere in our camp, I would prove myself as great an enemy of Texas as Santa Anna.

"Believe me, Hockley, in all our seven hundred-odd men, those that I can trust can be numbered on my two hands." And he spread his large hands in front of him. "If it's any comfort to you, you are among them. But with all our hotheads, so hungry for personal glory and so impatient with the processes of war, I cannot risk my plans being known."

Hockley gazed at the tall man's face and realized how fatigue and worry had etched deep lines in it since their arrival at Gonzales, six weeks before.

"Patience, Hockley. Patience and fortitude." The General turned and walked away.

Abruptly at three-thirty in the afternoon, Houston gave the orders for his men to form in fighting ranks. On the left were the first and second infantry regiments. In the center were the two cannons. On the right were the regulars and the cavalry. By Houston's count there were seven hundred eighty-three men in the line. Houston figured that Santa Anna had at least twice this number. What the Texans lacked in number, they must make up in surprise. Santa Anna, Houston was certain, had expected him to attack at dawn, as had most of his own men. Now he knew the Mexicans would be relaxed. They might even be taking afternoon siestas. The reinforcements that General Cos had brought would, he thought, be resting after their long forced march.

Houston rode his white stallion out in front of his lines, raised his sword and started to advance, riding back and forth in front of his men. Somewhere in the rear a flute and drum played "Come to the Bower," an old romantic ballad—not martial music but better than no music at all.

Men who remembered the words to the old ballad may have thought them strange for a battle song—

> *Will you come to the bower*
> *I have shaded for you,*
> *I have decked it with roses*
> *All spangled with dew.*

The cavalry on the right was moving rapidly. In the center the two six-pound cannons were pulled along through the tall and bright green grass, lurching now and then as they struck soft spots in the earth. The foot soldiers moved steadily forward, pushing the grass aside as they came, their rifles held in ready position across their chests. Some had pistols as well as rifles, and almost all had bowie knives stuck in their belts. The bright afternoon sun glinted on the newly-honed knife blades.

There was a shout from the west. Deaf Smith, his horse white with lather, came galloping up, waving an axe above his head as if it were a sword. In his strange, flat voice Deaf Smith shouted:

"I have cut down Vince's bridge. Now fight for your lives. Victory or death. Remember the Alamo!"

A murmur ran through the line of advancing men like wind running through the prairie grass. Some of them echoed Deaf Smith's cry: "Remember the Alamo!" If there had ever been any thought of escape, there was none now.

Houston, sensing the growing excitement, was afraid his men would fire too soon and be shot while they were reloading.

"Hold your fire, men!" he roared. "Hold your fire. Wait. Hold your fire!"

The Mexicans had piled saddles, gear and baggage to make a five-foot barricade from behind which they could fire in safety. The line of Texans, steady and silent, approached it.

Houston wheeled his white stallion when he was within twenty yards of the barricade, seized his wide beaver hat and waved it in the air. It was the signal.

The gun crew, with George Hockley in charge, whirled the two cannons around, pointing them toward the center of the Mexican barricade, and touched the fuses. The two cannons roared, almost in unison, and the charges of broken horseshoes, scrap iron, bolts and nails tore through the barricade and the Mexicans behind it.

"Now!" Houston roared, and the advancing infantrymen broke into a dead run toward the barricade, yelling like savages.

From behind the barricade came the cracking of rifles, the flames spitting out toward the rapidly advancing line. The infantrymen ignored this. Each rushed on to get close enough to put his one rifle shot to good account.

Houston was riding well in front of his men and the cannon. Suddenly his horse gave a shudder and a great sigh and blood spattered from his white chest. In the next instant Houston felt a tremendous blow on his leg, looked down and saw his foot dangling uselessly from the stirrup. Blood spurted from the torn boot.

He paid it no attention but wheeled his horse again, bearing his weight on one leg, and dashed toward the barricade. The foot soldiers were almost upon it. Now they stopped, carefully sighted along the long barrels and squeezed the triggers. Then, having no bayonets, they seized their rifles by the muzzles to use as clubs and sprang toward the barricade, screaming hoarsely, "Remember the Alamo, remember the Alamo!" And now someone added, "Remember Goliad!"

The Texans clubbed right and left with their rifle butts, smashing skulls, dashing rifles from the hands of the terrified Mexicans. Those who had pistols used them, and soon all were wielding their bowie knives, the broad blades glistening with blood in the afternoon sun.

Shouts were coming from the Mexicans now: "Me no Alamo! Me no Goliad!"

Deaf Smith had abandoned his axe and, seizing a sword, rode his horse hard for the line where the infantrymen were fighting hand to hand with the Mexicans. Just before he reached the line his horse stumbled. The celebrated scout was sent somersaulting through the air, landing squarely on his head in the midst of the fight. He had lost his sword. A Mexican drew back his bayonet for a thrust at Smith. Smith drew a pistol from his belt and pulled the trigger. The pistol missed fire. Smith threw the pistol with all his strength, hitting the Mexican in the head and knocking him out. Then Smith seized the man's rifle and plunged into the fight with the bayonet flashing.

As Houston had expected, Santa Anna was asleep when the attack began. Finally he dashed from his tent, wearing red carpet slippers and rubbing his eyes.

*They were a tangled mass of humans and horses*

He called a drummer to beat the drums and assemble the disorganized Mexicans. The drummer replied that he was shot. Santa Anna angrily shouted to a trumpeter to sound a blast on his horn. The trumpeter explained that he, too, was shot. Santa Anna saw one of his finest divisions, led by General Almonte, go streaming by in retreat. This was enough. He threw himself upon a big black horse and rode away as fast as the horse could carry him.

Now wild-eyed Americans were pursuing desperate Mexicans all over the plain. One group of Mexican cavalry sought to escape by Vince's bridge. They found, of course, that it had been destroyed. But their momentum carried them over the bank and in an instant they were a tangled mass of humans and horses, screaming, twisting and drowning in the deep bayou.

In less than twenty minutes the battle had turned into a rout and a slaughter. The Americans, many of whom had been peaceful farmers and had never fired a gun in anger, had become killers, maddened by the memory of what had happened to their fellowmen at Agua Dulce, San Patricio, the Alamo and Goliad.

Houston was weak from his wounds and the big white horse, losing blood rapidly, was beginning to stumble. Houston turned and rode back to the grove on Buffalo Bayou. Hockley was standing under the trees with the other officers. Hockley's face was black from firing the Twin Sisters. Houston rode slowly up to the men.

"Texas . . ." he started to say. The dying horse finally stumbled to the ground and Houston fell into Hockley's arms in a faint. He was stretched out under a live oak tree. A surgeon probed the shattered ankle for bits of broken bone.

The chase went on all night long, the Texans bringing in prisoners and spoils. The prisoners came in by the hundreds, and dead bodies littered the plain. The Texans, who had never had enough guns, powder or horses, now had all they could use, and more.

The next morning one search party was patrolling near the site of Vince's bridge. They came upon a

small, sad-faced Mexican, sitting on high ground looking dismally at the spot where the bridge had been.
He was wearing a strange blue smock, apparently
looted from a deserted farm house. And he was wearing red carpet slippers. The Texans thought he was
merely another Mexican. But when they brought him
back to the camp and prepared to put him in the prisoner's stockade, the other prisoners shouted:

*"El Presidente! Viva el Presidente!"*

The Texans stared at the little man. He drew himself
up and announced to his captors:

"Yes. I am General Antonio Lopez de Santa Anna.
You will please take me to General Houston."

Houston was still lying under the live oak tree. The
pain of his wound had kept him awake through the
night, and now he was dozing.

Santa Anna came up to the sleeping man and touched
his hand. Houston opened his eyes. They were glazed
with pain. The little man stepped back, drew himself
erect, placed his right hand over his heart and dramati-
cally extended his left hand.

"I am," he said, "General Antonio Lopez de Santa
Anna, President of Mexico. I claim to be your prisoner
of war."

Houston motioned to him to sit down on a box in
front of him and sent for an interpreter.

Santa Anna spurned the box, and, drawing himself

even more erect until he looked like a rooster ready to crow, said:

"That man may consider himself born to no common destiny who has conquered the Napoleon of the West."

Houston waved his hand wearily. Santa Anna continued:

*"I claim to be your prisoner of war," Santa Anna told Houston*

"It remains for such a man to be generous to the vanquished."

The glaze left Houston's eyes. Staring at the preposterous little man, he rumbled:

"You should have remembered that at the Alamo."

# 23: *The Young Republic*

WHAT SAM HOUSTON DID IN FORTY DAYS WAS A military miracle.

He had started with a handful of volunteers. They were frightened by war, as all honest men are. They were menaced by a highly trained and disciplined army at least twenty times their size. They were saddened by the brutal slaughter of their comrades and by the loss of their homes. They were distressed by lack of equipment and training. They were confused by contradictory commands. They were mystified by their leader who would not divulge his plans.

Houston had doubled the size of the group, kept

163

them together, trained them, disciplined them. With them he had confronted a large body of the enemy's picked troops, led by a self-confessed military genius, and fought the enemy to a standstill.

Later, historians ranked San Jacinto with the world's great decisive battles. Because of it and the events that followed it, the United States was to stretch across the continent to the Pacific, adding a million square miles, roughly one-third of its present area.

Little of this was apparent immediately after the battle.

Houston himself, through pain and loss of blood, was hardly aware of the situation.

The interim government, headed by President David Burnet, which had fled from Washington-on-the-Brazos to Harrisburg and thence to Galveston Island, was practically unaware of it. Burnet and his cabinet came to the San Jacinto battlefield to gather souvenirs, and one of President Burnet's few observations about the battle was that he understood General Houston had used profanity in achieving his victory.

Burnet did not like Houston and made no secret of it. He refused Houston passage on his boat returning to Galveston, although he later relented and allowed the wounded man to be carried aboard.

Houston needed expert surgery and the closest place

to get it was New Orleans. At Galveston a Texas naval captain, under Burnet's influence, refused him passage on a naval vessel. Houston was finally taken aboard a small and dirty trading vessel.

At New Orleans, he was the hero of the hour. Dirty, unkempt and ragged he was greeted by a tremendous crowd at the waterfront and cheered endlessly.

After a series of operations on his ankle he made his way back to Texas in June, traveling overland and still depending on crutches for support.

In Texas, meanwhile, confusion had grown. President Burnet had moved his fast-traveling government from Galveston to Velasco, and from Velasco to Columbia.

Burnet had concluded a treaty with Santa Anna which neither party obeyed. When Santa Anna was loaded on a vessel to return to Mexico the Texas army kidnapped him from the vessel, and for a time it appeared that the army might overthrow Burnet's government. Burnet also had lost the Constitution which the people were to vote upon.

When Burnet called for an election of officers of the new republic, Houston's name was advanced as a candidate. Houston, convalescing at the home of a friend in San Augustine, at first showed no interest in running and gave his supporters no encouragement; but just before the election in September, 1836, he wrote to a friend: "The crisis requires it or I would not have yielded. Duty, I hope, will not always require this sacrifice of my repose and quiet."

Houston won overwhelmingly, getting 5,119 votes to 743 for his closest rival. The voters also approved the new republic's constitution (a copy had been found by that time) and voted in favor of annexation to the United States. Few had ever wanted Texas to be anything more than a temporary republic.

There was strong sentiment for annexation in the United States, too. Southern senators and congressmen favored it. They thought Texas would enter as a slave-holding state and would increase the strength of the pro-slavery bloc in Congress. Many northerners favored it for the added military security it would give the western frontier, as well as the wealth of natural resources that would be added to the nation, but they feared the extension of slave territory.

President Jackson was in a peculiar position. He wanted Texas. He had tried to buy it from Mexico. But at the outset of the Texas revolution he had proclaimed the United States' neutrality; annexation of the new territory might be described as violation of that neutrality, and he did not want to risk war with Mexico.

Texas' only hope was to stand on her own legs as a

republic, demonstrate that she had a stable government and economy, capable of defending herself against Mexico. This Houston tried to accomplish as well as he could.

Houston took the oath of office in the crude frame capital at Columbia, standing before a table draped with a woolen blanket. "We are only in the outset of the campaign for liberty," he told his audience.

At the close, he grasped with both hands the sword he had carried at San Jacinto, held it aloft, and with a quavering voice said, "It now becomes my duty to make a presentation of this sword—this emblem of my past office. I have worn it with some humble pretensions in defense of my country; and should the danger of my country again call for my services, I expect to resume it and respond to that call, if needful with my blood and life."

Houston did not need his sword as president, but he needed everything else he had, including his cuff links. The new Republic of Texas had no seal to put on official documents. Houston's cuff links had a design of a dog's head and a rooster, with the motto "Try me." He would press a cuff link in the hot sealing wax on state papers, giving them an official air.

Houston moved the capitol from Columbia to the new town of Houston, newly laid out on the Buffalo

Bayou, not far from the San Jacinto battlefield. The president slept and worked in crude cabins and tramped the muddy streets like everyone else.

Stephen Austin, whom he had defeated for the presidency, became Houston's secretary of state but died soon afterward, dreaming in his last illness that Texas had been recognized by the United States. Of him Houston said, "The father of Texas is no more." Of different temperament, the two men agreed on important matters, and Austin had been Houston's ablest cabinet officer.

Of the various problems of starting a new government, one of the most serious was handling the army.

After the victory at San Jacinto recruits for the Texas army had come streaming in from all of the United States. Many of the recruits were simply adventurers. General Felix Huston from Mississippi was one of the late comers. He managed to work his way into command of the army, which by this time numbered about 2,500, three times the number with which Houston had won at San Jacinto.

Eager for glory and spoils, and with little else to do, Felix Huston agitated for a campaign against the Mexican town of Matamoros. Whenever soldiers could think of nothing better to do they planned a campaign against Matamoros.

Sam Houston knew the dangers of another conflict

with Mexico. Late one night when Felix Huston was away from the army's camp, he sent his secretary of war to the camp with orders furloughing all but 600 men in the army. By companies, the men were furloughed to various towns along the coast. Before Felix Huston returned the largest part of his army was scattered to the four winds. Felix Huston left soon afterward.

In more peaceful ways Houston organized the government and made it a going concern. Officers of the government were paid. Veterans of the war received promised grants of land. The population grew steadily as people flooded in from the east and north. Trade agreements were made with other nations. The new republic's money was made firm and valuable. Mail was delivered and customs collected on imports.

According to the constitution, the president could not succeed himself. When Houston's two-year term ended, his vice-president, Mirabeau Buonaparte Lamar, who had commanded the cavalry at San Jacinto, was elected president. A well-meaning but impractical man, Lamar was full of ambitious schemes. Through wild spending he let Texas currency drop to one-fifth of its former value, and he became involved in another dispute with Mexico that threatened to plunge Texas into war again.

Houston served in the Texas Congress while Lamar

was in office. He also traveled widely in the United States and everywhere he went he was hailed as a hero. In 1840 he re-married. His bride was Miss Margaret Lea of Alabama. Although much younger than her husband, Mrs. Houston made the old warrior happier than he had ever been before. With her encouragement Houston built a plantation called "Raven Hill" for his family.

Then in 1841 he ran again for the presidency, defeating his old enemy, David Burnet. Burnet scornfully referred to Houston as "half-Indian," while Houston called him a "hog thief."

Lamar had increased Texas' public debt from $190,000 to nearly five million dollars. Houston began rigid economies. He cut salaries in half, including his own. When one man tried to collect money the state owed him, Houston offered him instead half of everything he owned.

"What do you own?" the man asked.

"All I have in the world is an old, broken-down stallion that is eating his head off, and a game rooster without a hen to lay an egg."

When the Texas Congress voted him dictatorial powers, Houston vetoed it. He averted the new war with Mexico that Lamar had almost brought about. Meanwhile, he set in motion a train of events that ended in annexation to the United States.

Three factors served to change the attitude of the United States. Texas was becoming increasingly prosperous; her population had more than doubled. She concluded a truce with Mexico. And finally, she had become very friendly with Great Britain. The United States was not anxious to see British influence growing on her western frontier. James K. Polk, Democratic candidate for President of the United States in 1844, ran on a platform favoring annexation and was elected.

By the time the details of annexation had been worked out, Anson Jones, a doctor and secretary of state under Houston, had succeeded Houston as president.

On February 16, 1846, the Lone Star flag was run down from the capitol, which by this time had been moved to Austin, and the Stars and Stripes run up. Texas was the twenty-eighth state in the Union. As he watched the flags change, Anson Jones said:

"The final act in this great drama is now performed; the Republic of Texas is no more."

## 24: "My Country..."

SAM HOUSTON SERVED FOR THIRTEEN YEARS IN the United States Senate, representing the new state of Texas.

During that time his chief concern was the growing tension between North and South, over the slavery issue. He considered himself a southerner, but at all times he maintained that the Union was more important than any section of it, North or South, and that the South's threat of secession was wrong.

In Texas his views were not popular. Texas had been settled almost entirely by immigrants from the South, and the state's preponderant feeling was for the South.

In 1859 Houston returned to Texas and won the governorship. Although a majority disagreed with his views on secession, he was still a popular hero. Thousands of babies, a few steamboats and at least one railroad locomotive were named for him.

And on the twenty-fourth anniversary of the battle of San Jacinto, old soldiers gathered at the battlefield and urged Sam Houston to run as "the people's candidate" in the coming presidential election.

At the convention of the new National Union party in Baltimore, Houston's name was placed in nomination as a presidential nominee. "Give us this man," shouted a speaker, "whose blood once ran like water in defense of the Union . . . who fought the Indians when they were enemies and lived with them when they were friends; who has been a governor of two states; who has drawn his sword in defense of two republics; who has been president of one and is now on his way to that high office in the other. Give us this man . . . like old Jackson, who knows no party when enemies attack his beloved Union."

The speech was a fine tribute to Houston's full career, but it did not get him the nomination.

Popular hero or no, there was much feeling against him in Texas. In the new state capital of Austin one man had bragged that Sam Houston would not dare show his face in the streets.

Houston, nearing seventy years of age but still straight as a rifle barrel, smiled and walked the streets in search of the man. He found him in a hotel dining room, telling a group of listeners of Sam Houston's treachery and cowardice. Without a word the old man sat down across from the speaker and stared at him. The man's face turned red, but he did nothing.

Talk of secession from the Union was growing. Houston warned that Texas had not joined the South or the North but the Union. If the principle of secession were adopted and a southern nation formed, the principle of secession would permit the South to split again and again, forming a number of small, quarrelsome nations.

But secession talk kept on. Despite Houston's urging, a convention was called and it was decided to submit the question of secession to the people.

Houston began traveling around the state urging people to vote against secession. Frequently angry insults were shouted at him and at least once his life was threatened. But Houston kept in good humor and his wit was quick. Someone asked him what he honestly thought of a man who was, at the same time, making speeches in Texas in favor of secession. "He has every characteristic of a dog," Houston said, "except one—fidelity."

On one of the last of these speaking trips Houston was traveling north out of Austin in his old top buggy

*The rider handed Houston a letter from Abraham Lincoln*

with his Negro servant, Jeff Hamilton, driving. As they neared Belton they heard hoofbeats on the road behind them. Jeff pulled on the reins and stopped the big sorrel trotter.

The rider, his horse in a lather, dashed up and handed Houston a sealed envelope. Houston glanced at it, told Jeff to head back to Austin. In Austin he summoned members of his staff and read the letter to them. It was from Abraham Lincoln, who would, in the next two weeks, be inaugurated as President of the United States. Lincoln offered Houston a commission as a general in the Union army and said that if Houston would help keep Texas in the Union, he would send Union troops to Texas to help him. Houston asked his staff members what they thought. While they all felt as Houston did about secession, they believed that accepting Lincoln's plan would be a mistake.

Houston crumpled the letter and threw it in his office fireplace.

"I will do as you say," he said, "but if I were ten years younger I would not."

He continued to speak against secession, often facing hostile and threatening crowds. Few newspapers would print his speeches for fear of losing business.

But his efforts were in vain. The people of Texas voted three to one in favor of secession.

As a result, state officers were required to take an oath of allegiance to the Confederate States of America. Houston declined to do so and was forced out of the governorship. While the oath-taking was going on in the capitol, Houston sat on the porch of the executive mansion, a short distance away, enjoying the sunshine, listening to bird calls, admiring the new spring greenery on the capitol lawn, and whittling wooden toys for his children—swords for the boys, hearts for the girls. Mrs. Houston loaded the seven children into the family's old yellow coach and set off for their home in Huntsville. Houston and Jeff Hamilton followed in the old top buggy, pulled by Houston's favorite horse, Horseshoe, named for the battle of so many years before.

Of all the sad and painful roads that Sam Houston had traveled in his life—the road back from Tohopeka, the road from Tennessee to his exile among the Indians, the slow retreat across Texas from Gonzales—the road from Austin back to private life was the saddest. A public career that had lasted almost half a century was over.

The old General still made a few public appearances. He never stopped warning the people of Texas that secession and civil war could lead only to tragedy. But when his eldest son, Sam Jr., was preparing to march away, the old warrior reviewed the boy's regiment at Galveston. The old man wore the snuff-colored trousers he had worn at San Jacinto, and carried his San Jacinto sword tied with buckskin thongs. Although the young Confederate soldiers knew he was against the cause for which they were going to fight, they cheered him again and again.

Houston knew death was coming. He made a will, and in it left his San Jacinto sword to Sam, Jr., "to be drawn only in defense of the Constitution, the laws and liberties of his country. If any attempt should ever be made to assail one of these, I wish it to be used in its vindication."

Shortly before the old man died, Jeff Hamilton stopped and listened at the door of the room in which Houston lay.

"My country," he heard the dying man say, "oh, my country."

## 25: "Call It San Jacinto"

THE THREE OLD MEN SAT AND STARED AT THE FIRE.
It was burning low. Back of them the moon was rising
over the bottomlands of the Brazos River, the one the
Spaniards had named Rio de los Brazos de Dios,
River of the Arms of God. The moonlight silhouetted
a field of corn, just coming into tassel, growing tall in
the rich bottomland.

The old men talked, as old men do, of things they'd
talked over many times before.

"And when the fight was over," one was saying, "our
boys was chasing Mexicans all over that prairie. Some
was getting themselves a fine horse with a fancy Mexi-

can saddle or a good English musket or a sword. And some of us was just standing around under that mossy old live oak tree. Old Sam was laying there on the ground, a dirty shirt wrapped around his busted ankle. One of the Mexican generals was there, too, one that could talk American. He was asking Old Sam how we beat the daylights out of them that way.

"Old Sam he reaches in a pocket and pulls out an ear of dry corn. Part of the grains was gone. He wags it at this Mexican general and he says, 'Sir,' he says, he was always polite that way, 'Sir, how do you reckon you can ever lick men who fight for freedom and want it bad enough to march and fight with dry corn as rations?'

"Well, the boys all hoorayed, and one of them asks Old Sam if they can't have his ear of corn to keep. They'll plant it and call it Houston corn.

" 'Take it,' says old Sam, 'if it means anything to you. Divide it up and give each man a kernel as far as she'll go. Take it home and plant it in your fields and look after it just as you fought for your freedom today. Only don't call it for me. Call it for San Jacinty.'

"Old Sam was right. It growed right good. Taller than any other in Texas. Or anywhere else, I reckon."

# Index

181